Frederick
Philip Grove

CRITICAL VIEWS ON CANADIAN WRITERS

Frederick Philip Grove

Edited and with an Introduction by
DESMOND PACEY

MICHAEL GNAROWSKI, Series Editor

THE RYERSON PRESS
TORONTO WINNIPEG VANCOUVER

ISBN 0-7700-0314-1

PRINTED AND BOUND IN CANADA
BY THE RYERSON PRESS

CONTENTS

INTRODUCTION

A graph tracing the curve of Frederick Philip Grove's literary reputation would show a remarkably level line: he enjoyed no sudden leaps into fame, suffered no sudden falls into critical disfavour. When he began to publish his books, in the early nineteen-twenties, he was recognized at once for what he was: a mature man of wide and deep experience who brought to the production of Canadian literature an erudite mind and a practised sensibility that set him apart; when he died, as the three obituary tributes included in this book will show, he was respected rather than revered, soberly admired rather than enthusiastically loved. From first to last, his reputation was substantially confined to Canada: for a few years, from roughly 1928 to 1933, his books were reviewed also in the United Kingdom and the United States, but the reviews, though they were mildly favourable, were not sufficiently prominent or adulatory to make his name internationally famous. I believe it is true to say that, at home, Grove is regarded as Canada's greatest novelist; abroad his reputation does not begin to rival that of Hugh MacLennan, Morley Callaghan, Mordecai Richler or Leonard Cohen. When I recently visited some German universities in search of facts about Grove's early life, German professors of literature were prone to assume that it was Hugh MacLennan on whom I was working, since for them MacLennan is *the* Canadian novelist.

1

The evenness of Grove's reputation has been varied by only three slight peaks, one occurring in the late nineteen-twenties, one in the late nineteen-forties and one in the late nineteen-sixties. The occasion of the first of these peaks was the publication, between 1925 and 1933, of the five Grove novels which drew most attention—*Settlers of the Marsh* (1925), *A Search for America* (1927), *Our Daily Bread* (1928), *The Yoke of Life* (1930) and *Fruits of the Earth* (1933)—and the fact that, in 1928 and 1929, Grove made lecture tours across Canada under the auspices of the Association of Canadian Clubs and hence became something of a national celebrity. The second peak, if that is not too strong a word, was also the result of a combination of circumstances: the publication of my book on Grove in 1945 (a book which, in those days when Canadian books were few and far between, elicited several long review articles in the leading periodicals) and the publication of Grove's autobiography, *In Search of Myself,* in 1946. Most recently, there has been an upsurge of interest in Grove occasioned by the publication of Professor Spettigue's book, and particularly by its suggestion that Grove's own autobiography was largely a work of fiction rather than of fact.

The result of Professor Spettigue's revelations — he demonstrates that there is no Castle Thurow in southern Sweden, no record of a Grove family in that area, and that the Grove who sailed from Hamburg to America in 1892 was a small boy rather than a young man—is almost certain to be to focus scholarly attention, for the next few years, on Grove's biography. I cannot quarrel with that development, having independently developed an interest in the question myself since I began, two or three years ago, to prepare an edition of Grove's letters, but I do hope that the detective zeal involved in biographical investigation will not preclude some attention being paid to the critical examination of the work rather than the man.

That serious and lively critical examination of the work

is needed is, I believe, the chief lesson to be drawn from the material that follows. With very rare exceptions, the critics who have addressed themselves to Grove's work have done so superficially and repetitively. Between them, the first two critics to look at a group of Grove's books, Raymond Knister and Robert Ayre, said almost everything that has been said since, whether in praise or blame.

Knister's essay dates itself rather badly by its strident cultural nationalism, but once we have got past that barrier we find most of the essential general points being made: that Grove's "language is often abstract and the characters not fully visualized," that essays seem to be a more natural form of expression to him than novels, and that Grove is a writer who combines power of expression and fidelity of observation with something "downright awkward and childish."

The few points that Knister failed to make in 1928 were almost all made by Robert Ayre in 1932. Ayre saw Grove as "a man of the past," "rooted in Europe," a scholar and philosopher who studied the life of the Canadian West but did not fully comprehend it. It was Ayre who first gave currency to the image of Grove as a serious, ponderous writer whose "profundity can thicken into turgidity," who is kept down by pedantry, who is too much the schoolmaster and too little the artist. It was Ayre too who first uttered the criticism that has been repeated *ad nauseam* ever since—that Grove could not portray living human beings, that he lacked passion and emotional spontaneity: "His beauty is the austere beauty of the mind rather than the warm beauty of the senses"; "Sometimes it seems as if Grove is against life. There is something disconcerting in his obsession with purity."

Isabel Skelton's essay, published in 1939, is largely a rehearsal of the adverse criticisms made by Knister and Ayre; indeed she even denies to Grove some of the virtues which they had allowed him. Ayre and Knister had noted admiringly the patient fidelity with which Grove describes the minutiae of Nature; Mrs. Skelton alleges that these descriptions are often overdone. To their charges that he was deficient in vitality of characterization and in passionate involvement in life she adds charges of her own: that many of his more sensational scenes are unreal and incredible, that he is unable to deal convincingly with sex, that his prairie novels have little value as social documents and that he lacks a satisfying philosophy of life. So embracing are her strictures, indeed, that one is compelled to wonder why she felt such an author was worthy of a long critical essay.

Looking back on my own book on Grove twenty-five years later, I see its chief value as demonstrating that Grove indeed had, if not a "satisfying" philosophy of life, at least a consistent one. For that reason, and because the book is now out of print, I have decided somewhat reluctantly to reprint below the chapter in that book on Grove's tragic vision. The biographical chapters were of some interest when they appeared, but since they were avowedly merely a summary of Grove's autobiography, then in manuscript, they lost virtually all their value when *In Search of Myself* was published in 1946. It is embarrassing for me to find, in the light of Professor Spettigue's diligent researches, that the names and dates in those chapters were dubious at best, completely false at worst. That I accepted Grove's version of his life at face value was probably proof of my naiveté—but I think I am still naive enough to assume that if a man volunteers to tell his own life story, and especially if he proves willing to answer questions put to him about that story, the story is basically true. As a matter of fact I am still prepared to argue that Grove's account of his life is substantially true, and have evidence for this view which I hope to bring forward at the appropriate time—but that Grove fictionalized the names of persons and places I must reluctantly concede.

The inaccuracy of the biographical chapters of that book bothers me less, however, than the weakness of the chapters in which I essayed to make critical appraisals of Grove's novels. I was at that time, as a result of my work at Cambridge on the influence in late Victorian England of French realism and naturalism, completely wedded to the realistic theory of the novel. As almost all other critics of Grove have been, I was content to apply to his novels the usual realistic canons of credibility, consistency, social accuracy and psychological objectivity. I failed to see—and to this day no one has fully demonstrated—that Grove is as much a surrealist as a realist, and that an examination of his patterns of imagery and symbolism would have been much more revealing than my rote application of the rules of Flaubert and Zola.

Because I failed properly to assess the nature of Grove's art, but was relatively successful in seeing in clear outline Grove's underlying philosophy, the net effect of my book was to suggest that Grove was a defective artist but a powerful thinker. This effect can be clearly seen in B. K. Sandwell's essay: when Sandwell says that "In spite of his deficiencies of style and structure . . . Grove is by far the greatest philosophical literary artist to emerge as yet in Canada," he is neatly summarizing my book's main, if somewhat misguided, theme.

An attempt at a far more penetrating artistic appraisal of Grove's work was made in 1946 by Professor W. E. Collin in his article "La Tragique Ironie de Frederick Philip Grove" (*Gants du Ciel*, IV, 15-40). After prolonged debate I have decided not to include that essay in this book: it is long, involved and, as a whole, a failure; in individual insights it is brilliant, but these brilliant passages mean little when detached from their setting. It reads as if Collin had glimpsed a truth about Grove which he found himself unable to express. In an unpublished address which Professor Collin later delivered before Section II of the Royal Society of Canada, an examination of symbolic patterns in Grove's unpublished and unfinished novels, he did indeed find the words to express his sense of Grove's achieved complexity—unfortunately Professor Collin was unable to provide me with the text of this address. But Collin, I am convinced, was on the right track: he saw Grove not as a realist but as an ironist, not as a naturalistic but as a ritualistic novelist.

Professor E. A. McCourt's chapter on Grove in his *Canadian West in Fiction* (1949), on the other hand, represents a sensible and orderly synthesis of existing views on Grove rather than a breakthrough into originality. McCourt takes up the by then established notions of Grove's limitations: his "incomplete understanding of men and women," his excessive intellectuality and insufficient emotionality, his lack of the novelist's *donnée* of passionate commitment to life. Picking up from Collin the notion that Grove's characters are symbols rather than individuals, McCourt sees this not as a possible source of strength (as I am sure Collin saw it) but as a weakness: "Symbols, no matter how ingeniously created, are in the end lifeless things." Are Ahab and Moby Dick, to mention no others, so completely lacking in life? Disregarding the sincere compassion so evident in Grove's treatment of John Elliot and Len Sterner, McCourt asserts that "Grove rarely, if ever, felt warmly towards any human being" and echoes Knister in arguing that Grove was by temperament an essayist rather than a novelist: "The tragedy of his artistic life is that so much of his work was done in a medium for which he had little talent. His best bits of writing are descriptive and philosophical rather than narrative."

Professor A. L. Phelps' essay on Grove, in his *Canadian Writers* (1951), is chiefly interesting for its first-hand glimpses of Grove the man and for its assertion that Grove's failure to reach a wider readership was attributable to the weakness of Canadian criticism. This latter idea is expanded upon in Wilfrid Eggleston's 1957 essay: Grove "was handicapped in failing to find in time friendly critics and editors who might have helped him greatly to attain virtuosity in literary style." Now there may be some truth in the view that Grove was failed by his critics, but I do not think their failure consisted in not drawing attention to the occasional awkwardnesses in Grove's style. Their failure—and it was my failure too—was a failure to grasp the nature of Grove's symbolic art. Grove himself was given to complaining about his critics, but what he complained about, and I think now with justice, was that they never seemed to understand what he was trying to do.

One of the most challenging assertions in Wilfred Eggleston's essay is that Grove's "most perfect work . . . is almost certainly to be found in his nature essays, his short stories, his literary criticism and his lyrics. His most perennially interesting work is to be found in his two books of autobiography." I cannot accept that statement unreservedly, but in some ways it is prophetic. There are in existence over seventy of Grove's short stories, of which only half a dozen or so have been accessibly published, and when a selection of the best of them appears it should establish the fact that Grove is a far greater master of the short story form than has hitherto been believed. And if Professor Spettigue is right, and Grove's "autobiographies" are not autobiographies in the usual sense at all, but rather works of fiction, they will indeed be perennially interesting. To live an exciting life may be much, but to invent an exciting life with such verisimilitude that people will accept it as sober truth for a whole generation may well be more.

Having reviewed the longer essays in this book, I do not intend to review the reviews, except in the most general terms. What impresses me with the reviews, in the light of Grove's own and other people's allusions to the failure of Canadian criticism to appreciate his work, is their generally sympathetic and perceptive nature. All of his books had a good press, and if they did not become best-sellers it was not because reviewers ignored or damned them. Even *Settlers of the Marsh*, which Grove alleged was attacked by the reviewers for its obscenity, was in fact given a very respectful reading—and, indeed, most of the reviews that I have discovered make a point of defending the book's morality.

We are fond in this country of damning the reviewers in the daily press and of declaring that the only good criticism is to be found in the university quarterlies and the quality magazines. In Grove's case, it seems to me, the newspaper reviewers came much closer to doing what might reasonably be expected of them than did the academic critics. We do not expect criticism in depth from a newspaper review: we expect only that it provide us with some idea of what the book is about and with some tentative judgment whether the book is worth reading. This, in most cases, the newspaper reviews of Grove's books achieved. Of the academic critical essay, however, we expect some insight into the complexity of an author's thought and style—but of this kind of penetrating interpretation and appraisal Grove has so far received singularly little. I trust that the readers of this book, most of whom will be students, will realize the opportunity that this paucity of thoroughgoing critical analysis provides them.

Desmond Pacey

University of New Brunswick
December, 1969

GENERAL ESSAYS IN CRITICISM

A CANADIAN OF CANADIANS

RAYMOND KNISTER

In the development of America one of the most curious of phenomena is the fervour—the completely and practically manifested patriotism, of adoptive citizens. We are speaking here of what may be called the genuine article, not of the self-complacency of the immigrant who has made his pile in this country, genuine as it may be and worthy as he may be. And one of the most outstanding cases of this, one that could not be more genuine, is that of Frederick Philip Grove, who was born and "educated" for the most part, in Europe, and who is now and has been for a score of years or more, a Canadian of Canadians.

In contradistinction to the many able and well-equipped men who have come from Europe to play a part in this country, Mr. Grove's whole bent, his utmost energies, appear to have been directed to making himself a Canadian, making others Canadians, all to the glory of Canada with whose possibilities he became enamoured. Thus he stands out even among the artists and writers upon whom the spiritual leadership of the country depends; and his books, aside from purely literary considerations, have an immediate value and interest which can scarcely be estimated justly.

As to the books themselves, they number five: *Over Prairie Trails*, (1922); *The Turn of the Year*, (1923); *Settlers of the Marsh*, a novel, (1926);[1] *A Search for*

"Frederick Philip Grove" by Raymond Knister, in *Ontario Library Review* XIII, 3 (1928), 60-62. By permission of the Estate of Raymond Knister.
[1] This is an error. The novel first appeared in 1925. Ed.

America, (1927); *Our Daily Bread,* a novel, (1928). To get some idea of what manner of man Grove is, we should consider first *A Search for America,* as it deals with the early life of its author, and in particular and most exhaustively with his Americanization. His family was a Swedish-Scottish one, of wealth, and he was given every advantage of luxury and of training. The youth responded to this culture with an ambition to "master nothing less than all human knowledge." Thus though his energies were scattered, and he became something of a man about town—a somewhat Faustian one, it is to be presumed—he was not idle. He says of this period:

My work lacked simply that measure of co-ordination which might have made it useful for the purpose of earning a living when the necessity arose. I mastered, for instance, five modern languages, wrote an occasional tract in tolerable Latin, and read Homer and Plato with great fluency before I was twenty-two. I dabbled in Mathematics and in Science, and even attended courses in Medicine. Theology and Jurisprudence were about the only two fields of human endeavour which I shunned altogether.

At the age of twenty-four, when he was reaching a position to gratify his ambitions, his family suddenly lost its wealth. For some time he endeavoured to continue his studies together with his habits of a young man about town (he knew some of the greatest artists and writers of Paris rather as a patron than as a student) but the two roles would not be combined, and he decided to emigrate to America. Thus we find him landing at Montreal, a slim youth of over six feet in height, with the Scandinavian fairness, with the diffidence of the stranger and the courteous bearing of one accustomed to dealing with his inferiors—and with almost no money. Obviously, an interesting time awaits him.

It is in Toronto that his search for work is rewarded finally with a position as busboy in a restaurant, from which he is promoted to waiter. As soon as he had risen to the height of this profession he was induced, partly by the mendacity of a fellow-waiter, to go to New York. The episode of the waitership is described at length, and the difference in manners of European and American indicated (here everybody, even the friendly ones, seemed bent on "rubbing it in"); also the difference in *mores*: his fellow waiters were not above graft. He perceives, to his own alarm, a great truth regarding the relation of the immigrant to crime:

Hunger, despair, and helpless loneliness are strange prompters. I had begun to think less harshly of him who sins against society. . . . The path of the immigrant is sown with temptation: temptation of a spiritual kind—he is tempted to charge all his troubles to some incomprehensible vice in the very constitution of the new country or the new society into which he came. His need and distress may become extreme. If he sins, the society against which he sins is foreign to him, just as truly as he is foreign to it. What he sees of American morals is often, too often, not what shows them at their best.

A steady sense of values is needed by the average immigrant to maintain his integrity in the face of such conditions as are found in Canada, not to mention the cities of the United States, where the causes of foreign delinquency require such study.

In New York Mr. Grove became a book-agent, selling cheap "sets." But he was not a successful canvasser, because his conscience forbade his closing a sale when he felt that the prospective customer could not afford to buy the books. This difficulty was overcome when he began selling sets at fifteen hundred dollars and up to moneyed men; but after varied adventures alone and in sales team throughout the country, he discovers that this is nothing less than a swindle: the cheap sets have been merely rebound to sell at the exorbitant figures.

The section which follows is called The Depths, and in it we find Mr. Grove hoboing about the southern states and the ranches of the Mississippi River. He was quite destitute, except for the things the river brought him: one day a large tea kettle, the next a pumpkin, corn, a well preserved ham which in his state of ill-health made him ill. Few people does he meet in his wanderings now. One hermit keeps him a day or two to get over his illness, and says no word until Grove mentions that it is about time for him to be moving. Then he says: "I reckon."

Finally his health breaks, but providentially he falls into the hands of a country doctor who calls in specialists and at length puts him on his feet with a job. But there follow more wanderings, riding on the rods of trains, work as a harvest hand, before he settles and finds his niche. It is a story which is not only typical of America, but in a sense universal.

None the less the book is not wholly successful. With a wonderful mass of material, and with the greatest sincerity and impartiality, there is shown a lack of artistic power which is all the more strange and almost impossible at first to define. One comes to the conclusion that the author depends, as nearly all the autobiographers in history have done, upon the fact that his story is true, and does not devote enough pains to making it seem true. Thus many a tawdry romance of an underworld the authors have never seen, will appear truer than Grove's story, in its rendering. Possibly the very wealth of the material, the wealth of erudition of the author, has made simple directness and concreteness more difficult. The language is often abstract and the characters not fully visualized. But on the whole, lacking this artistic perfection which is the rarest thing in biography, the book is a notable one.

A Search for America occupies in Grove's experience only the first two or three years which he spent on this continent. He finally took up the profession of teaching in Manitoba, to which he has been devoted more or less ever since, for a score of years. A more valuable person for the Canadianization of foreign-born children would be hard to find. All the time he was writing, and in 1922 his first book was published, *Over Prairie Trails*. The present reviewer finds this the most satisfactory book which Mr. Grove has given us. It is not a novel, nor is it even meant to form a connected narrative. Yet it has an epic zest and largeness which is the rarest of qualities. It is the story of winter drives over the prairie which Grove made every weekend from the place where he taught school to the town where his wife and his little girl lived, and where the former also taught. The drives were some thirty miles each way, and the trail was for the most part difficult and almost impassible with snow. Two horses pulled the cutter, Peter and Dan; they deserve a place with Black Beauty and all the horses pictured in fiction. But Mr. Grove's whimsical naturalism in picturing these horses is surpassed by his comprehensiveness, his grasp of the whole sweep and of the smallest of minutiae of the prairie. In this respect he is truly unrivalled. There is no mood of the weather, no weed or flower or grass which escapes him. He is convinced that the kingdom of heaven lies all around us and his book is "like a botany book on fire," as Professor Phelps says in his introduction to the volume which followed it, *The Turn of the Year*. There is of course the eloquence of the devotee of "Nature," but it is based upon the naturalism of the observer, the man of erudition to whom everything is interesting. And underlying these things are the human values: will he succeed in making this heroic drive to meet his wife and child? Often in the account of these very real blizzards, with their shifting trails, their desolation, the prairie horses chasing ahead of his team, loth to get off the trail and sink in the deep snow, the cold, the silence, while "stripped of all accidentals, the universe swings on its way," the anxiety—often it looks as though the destination will not be reached. And once, on the last trip of the book, he does stop at a farmhouse halfway, to continue in the morning. *Over Prairie Trails* is a superb evocation of the prairie winter, sketched in appropriately huge strokes.

The Turn of the Year is not so successful. Its material is more various, consisting of essays and sketches of western life with emphasis on natural phenomena; but it is lacking in the unity and force which characterized the first book. It does remind one, however, of what a beautiful novel Mr. Grove could write with characters suited to the atmosphere he can paint so well, and with the place made into one of the characters.

It is surprising in that case to find Mr. Grove's novels on the whole so unsatisfactory. *Settlers of the Marsh* is powerfully conceived, the honesty and forthright intentions of the author are apparent, yet the book as a whole misses that finality of effect which it should have. In some instances it is downright awkward and childish, as when every few pages we are shown the depravity of the "fallen woman" the hero has married by the fact that she plasters her face with powder. One cannot help conclude that the novel is a strange harness to Mr. Grove's talent. He has to leave so many things unsaid, and forego the advantage of so many branches of his varied learning, that the finished novel must seem a very fragmentary thing.

The same things hold true to a lesser degree of *Our Daily Bread*, Mr. Grove's latest novel, just published. The conventions of novel-writing have taken so much of his attention that the novel itself seems to have been less fully conceived than, one feels sure, it was. We have here the prairie farmer, the pioneer, and his fate. His own seed turn aside from what has been his great purpose. . . .

With this theme, as fine as any presented to the novelist, Mr. Grove has not been wholly successful. He writes faithfully, he knows what he is writing about, one feels that he knows the characters from birth. But the combination of the whole fails to glow. *Our Daily Bread* is a book which deserves and will get a wide reading, and while it is not that prairie novel which we expect Mr. Grove will give us, his work as a whole is a definite contribution to Canadian tradition.

A SOLITARY GIANT

ROBERT AYRE

Frederick Philip Grove is a solitary giant, treading his own lonely trail, heedless of his contemporaries, unhurried, undistracted. If the analogy be not pressed too closely, he might be called the Theodore Dreiser of Canada; these two austere spirits, these two men with the clumsy tongues, have much in common. But when Dreiser stands in the streets to feel the currents of modern American life, Grove shrinks from them and gives himself to the slow rhythms of the grudging prairie; he does not belong to the New World.

It is true that Frederick Philip Grove turned his back on Europe many years ago and shouldered the heavy burden of the pioneer in a new country, but he remains rooted in Europe and in the past. The America he has chosen belongs more to cold, northern Europe than to the exuberant New World. He came to Canada because it was like his own Scandinavia, because in the United States he could not find the environment which would help him express the "individual tragic reaction to life" which is the fibre of his soul. In spite of "aberrations . . . from the ancient paths," he feels that Europe is still seeking after "the higher things of life," looking to the past when America jostles toward the future, and he is satisfied that when the United States abandoned itself to material gods Canada remained sober, European.

Some of us have less faith in Europe and the past. We are not so sure of ourselves today, we who have been tricked, we who repudiate the certainties of our fathers

---

"Frederick Philip Grove," by Robert Ayre. *Canadian Forum*, 12 (April, 1932), 255-7. By permission of Robert Ayre.

that have been shattered about our ears, we who know Science as a conjuror turning the universe inside and out, a handkerchief — there is nothing in it — and suddenly revealing God like a glass of water, only to make him disappear again. For all we know, two and two may be five; we are not so confident of our ability to discern "the higher things of life"; we may even have a suspicion that Tragedy itself is a sort of august Romanticism. But Grove belongs to a generation that was sure of itself. There is nothing new under the sun, says Grove, undisturbed alike by social upheavals and the revelations of the conjuror. Don't bother me. Society is always in eruption. What have we to learn from sleight-of-hand, from the frettings of your Freuds, Einsteins, Pirandellos?

It is inevitable that the forms we are coming to think are most successful in capturing Proteus are to him so many fads and fancies; it is to be expected that he would put his trust in the Greeks, in Goethe and Hardy, rather than in such as James Joyce, Virginia Woolf, and William Faulkner. What we have to ask ourselves is, how does he fulfil himself in the old forms?

He has led us to expect much of him. As a man of the past, he possesses his creed and he has confessed himself to us abundantly, in magazine articles, in his series of lectures *It Needs to Be Said,* in all his books. We are bound to respect a writer who has the strength to keep his feet firmly on the straight path, who sees his purpose shining as the Holy Grail and gives his life to the following of it. There is something heroic in such a man. His devotion and his resoluteness, his honesty with himself and the world make criticism seem mere carping. Grove shuns what he considers the transient, and keeps his eyes fixed on the Great Tradition, unshaken by "the clamor of the frantic public"; he labours seriously, almost grimly, for power, depth, and beauty; he offers us meat and bread instead of the sweetish custard he says the childish mind demands. "It is the universal verdict of mankind at its highest," he lays down, "that the feeling released in the human soul by the contemplation of life is tragic; and therefore, by inference, that human life itself is a tragic thing," and he sets out "not to distract but to lead the reader into the inner recesses of his soul."

Grove is a serious writer, so serious, indeed, as to be his own undoing. To a deep experience in reading, he adds a deep experience in living, and his books are the reactions of a serious mind. But profundity can thicken into turgidity and when Grove's performance falls short of his promise, it is because he stifles life. And it does fall short. The world asks more of its interpreters than high ideals and good intentions, and if we are bound to respect Grove for his integrity we are bound to be disappointed when he seems to fail.

Power, depth, and beauty Grove has achieved in his three novels, *Settlers of the Marsh, Our Daily Bread* and *The Yoke of Life*. In a measure, we feel there is something important here, but something is lacking. Grove withholds. Like the hard land he writes about, he yields slowly and grudgingly.

In the first place, his language hampers him. When the books come to life, it is in spite of his words. He does not infuriate us, as Dreiser can, but—he confesses it in *A Search for America*—he still smacks of the "English of fashionable governesses" and is rigid in his "peculiar stiffnecked lack of condescension to everyday slang." How can he create living people by "correcting" their speech, as he admits he does? He talks about his characters in stilted phrases and featureless clichés—the virtue of the best new writers is that they give their people liberty to illumine themselves—and he stuffs stilted language like oatmeal into their mouths. A novelist must have a light hold on reality when he self-consciously puts current usages, when he allows them, into quotation marks. Pedantry keeps Grove down. Thick, dead words. Life lies buried under them.

But dead words are only an outward manifestation of the pedantry that stifles. How we long for the intensity of a Lawrence to make the lives of these homesteaders real! How we miss, in these novels, the smell of hay and the feel of cool rain on the cheek! Neither for good nor ill, can Grove be called a novelist of "The Soil." "I love Nature more than man," he tells us in *Over Prairie Trails,* but in his novels Nature gets short shrift. He is out of place in the city, his city people are drawn with an unpractised hand, he cannot swing into the quicker tempo of the city: he is more at home with the simple country people, chiefly with the pioneers beyond the fringes of old-established settlement: but the land does not pervade his novels. Not in any of them does the prairie enter as a presence, as a doom, as might be said of the heath in *The Return of the Native*; never does the union of man and land become charged with passion as in *The Rainbow.* The bitter struggle of the Elliots in *Our Daily Bread* is a true story, but the struggle is not so much against an obstinate soil as against an abstract thing called Debt; and yet the Elliots cannot exist apart from the earth, as they seem to do when Grove, probably feeling that he would lower himself to Romanticism by so doing, refuses to allow the land to become a living character.

He need not deny the senses in his search for eternity, not if he is dealing with men and women, for surely when Adam delved the sweat stood on his brow and there was a rich warm smell to the earth he turned up; and if the men of the future will have no blood in their veins, what is the use of writing for posterity? But while he emphasizes its importance, the lyric eludes him. His beauty is the austere beauty of the mind rather than the warm beauty of the senses, the beauty of contours rather than colours. It may be true that art "converts the concrete fact into a spiritual experience which has eternal life," but is it not also true that a man is a sentient being and that you cannot define "the emotional attitude of man to that which is not he," nor "lead the reader into the inner recesses of his soul" except by way of the senses?

Sometimes it seems as if Grove is against life. There is something disconcerting in his obsession with purity. It is one of his ideals to stand aloof from his people, to be coldly, severely, "classic," neither to praise nor condemn; but the fact remains that, consciously or unconsciously, he takes a moral attitude; the didactic schoolmaster keeps rising up, like a spectre. We are disturbed by the wry comedy of Niels Lindstedt in *Settlers of the Marsh,* but we resent the stiff, childish morality involved in it. Is the fact that he belongs to the slowly maturing North excuse enough for Niels? Is the Tragic Reaction to life to be founded on the fumbling of adolescence? Niels, a grown man, is a virgin violated; his conscience forces him to marry the harlot who rapes him; his conscience forces him one day to murder her. He revenges himself on life. Len Sterner, in *The Yoke of Life,* a finer Niels, kills himself and Lydia because the girl had become a harlot. Mrs. Elliot, in *Our Daily Bread,* reveals the horrible secret that she had actually enjoyed the pleasures of marriage, and her sudden wild fling at the dance, just before her death, is hushed up and, for the sake of sobriety, a diabolically comic scene is suppressed. But Grove's genius is not for comedy.

The inner meaning of Len's union in death with Lydia is that a sensitive man cannot live without ideals and must die rather than suffer his ideals to be smirched, but surely this, too, is a denial of life.

Yet we know that life lies glowing underneath, because often it is fused to incandescence. The unforgettable figure of the patriarch Elliot, driven to his old home by a last light flaring up in his dimming brain. The episode of the driftwood fisher in *A Search for America* who said, "I reckon." Kolm's selling his potatoes to the Jew to get a dollar for young Len Sterner on his way to the lumber camp. The struggle for the horses in the slough, and the search after the hailstorm for the lost calf. The moment when Lydia burns the tent and deliberately accepts her doom, a flash of life before the dark. These are memorable passages. And we have *Over Prairie Trails* and *The Turn of the Year*.

Grove begins with *A Search for America*, carries on his experience in *Over Prairie Trails* and *The Turn of the Year*, and then develops into the three novels. *A Search for America* is the fascinating story of a young immigrant and his reactions to a new country. Its importance to us lies in its giving us the background of Grove himself. Frankly, it is the story of an individual and not the common experience of the immigrant, the story of a serious-minded youth, so earnest and unsophisticated as to make us incredulous of his gay life in the capitals of Europe; but because he is a conscientious, self-conscious young man, looking for a corner of the earth to plant his roots in, he examines other lives and institutions and the book therefore takes on a social significance all autobiographies do not possess. Bus boy, waiter, book agent, veneer man, tramp, hobo, farm hand—so he learned America, and it makes an entertaining and sometimes thrilling story. At least, to help foreign immigrants "build their partial views of America into total views . . . to assist them in realizing their promised land," he becomes teacher, doctor, lawyer, business agent, in the new settlements. The individual becomes the social man.

But never fully the social man, and this Grove confesses is the problem of the writer, the paradox of needing human contacts and solitude at the same time.

Over Prairie Trails and *The Turn of the Year* are the diaries of a solitary man. He is something of an heroic figure, this country teacher, driving his team under the stars, fighting the blizzard and the snowdrifts, or racing the hailstorm. The loneliness of the wife and child in the wilderness is touching and the father's dogged determination to be with them once a week, no matter what the weather, although he has miles to drive, becomes drama. So much that is lacking in the novels is to be found in the pages of these two simple books! The feeling of the wide, harsh plains which demand so much of this unbending man enters like iron. Too often, the writer is the scientific observer rather than the poet, and the pictures of snow and fog lose much by being so studied, but there is a swing, and something exultant in the man's determination and exertion; there is here the beauty of strength. The winds and snows of *Over Prairie Trails,* which is all winter, make us long for the wild geese and the coming of summer.

Over Prairie Trails ripens into *The Turn of the Year,* the most satisfying of all Grove's books. In form it has the beauty of a symphony; the cycle of the seasons revolves with the cycle of human lives. It has no purple passages: these would suit neither Grove nor the prairies, but not so often here is he the pedant, and he rises to urgent, honest poetry, the exultation a strong man. He comes close to the earth; we can smell it and feel it and, without falling sentimental, he evokes homesickness in the heart of the prairie-born. Why is all this withheld from his novels? *The Turn of the Year* is alive with the drama of the changing seasons, the thrill of the coming spring, the adventure of the stormy going down into winter. True to his own spirit, Grove makes winter the climax, but it is a manly surrender. The men and women are more substantial than in his novels: they are sweaty, real people. But at the same time, they rise up large and symbolic. John and Ellen, the Sower and the Reaper, they stand for the enduring earth. There is more tragedy in the half-dozen pages of the Icelandic Sower's story than in the whole of *Our Daily Bread.* We should have a new edition of *The Turn of the Year,* one, perhaps, that combines with it *Over Prairie Trails,* illustrated with good sturdy woodcuts, an edition worthy of a permanent work. This is the sort of book that should be reprinted season after season. Yes, we are persuaded for an hour to forget the conjuror. For in the long run, no matter how we approach it, there is always the earth, always storm and calm, the sky, the snow and the rain, always the Sower and the Reaper, always love and birth and growing old and passing into sleep.

ONE SPEAKING INTO A VOID

ISABEL SKELTON

When broadcasting on Canadian literary criticism, Frederick Philip Grove said that a writer whose work met no critical response was as one speaking into a void, "uncertain to whose capacity to adjust his utterance." Then in an article in the *University of Toronto Quarterly*, for July, 1938, he reveals his estimation of the Canadian "void" into which his own writings have fallen for many years. Mr. Grove states that his "better books" (this of course is his own ranking of them) remain unknown, while his second best have been successful for wholly irrelevant reasons. Such results have come about, he considers, because his public is "ignorant, cowardly and snobbish . . . and a non-conductor of any sort of intellectual current."

When an author frequently spoken of as "one of the small company of Canadian writers of the first order," and who has given "forty years of endeavour" to interpreting Canadian life in Canadian fiction, has come to such a painful conclusion about his readers, it is high time some one of them would try, as clearly as is possible in a few magazine pages, to indicate why his Canadian public prefer the books of his they do prefer, and to show that there may be some reasons found for their choice other than "ignorance," "cowardice," etc. It is always possible that the subject matter and its interpretation, together with the

"Frederick Philip Grove" by Isabel Skelton, in *Dalhousie Review* XIX (July, 1939), 147-163). By permission of *Dalhousie Review*.

style of the writing, may have an important part in the forming of the public verdict on any given book. It may turn out that the public recognize a truth and beauty in his better books (according to their ranking of them) which they find lacking in others, quite irrespective of the time and labour the author spent upon them. Or it may be that there is a repetition of material; in which case his public naturally chooses the book giving it with the least wayward bias, or philosophic ponderosity, or accumulation of prosaic facts. In other words, it is time to find out why the public like his things they like, and what they are.

Frederick Philip Grove's first published books, *Over Prairie Trails* (1922) and *The Turn of the Year* (1923), are a fitting overture to all his writings. In them are heard his dominating themes and sentiments. The subject-matter of the first is found in seven intimate drives the author with us, his readers, takes "in the southern fringe of the great northern timber expanse"—a district which later affords a setting for various parts of his novels. We shall not have accompanied Mr. Grove very far before we discover we are on no expedition to get acquainted with our fellow-men, or to take any cognizance of them. We shall have no genial give and take, passing the time of day with residents or fellow-travellers, no humorous stories or sad tales connected with this one or that one we meet. On the contrary, we find ourselves taken up, as it were, into a travelling hermitage and enjoying a holiday away from our kind.

When on one unfortunate occasion our driver's nerves had become broken, and it was necessary for him to spend the night at a farm by the road, the incident requires only the following space:

I drove into the yard of the farm where I had seen the light, knocked at the door, and asked for and obtained the night's accommodation for myself and for my horses.

At six o'clock next morning I was on the road again.

That ends that.

To gain more specific ideas as to what Mr. Grove gives and does not give, let us place beside this little interruption of a night's hospitality, as it drops out of his story, the way it would be taken up into Mr. W. H. Blake's *Brown Waters*, for example. It would have afforded Mr. Blake an opportune peg for a genial anecdote or for a "homey" picture of the inhabitants of that farm on that stormy night, or for some curious local legend or family history revealing the outlook of the people and passing into his possession through this accidental visit; and finally, next morning, when again we were on the road with him, it would have been with backward turning thoughts. In some way or other, the response of these people to the extra work which had been thrown upon them at the close of a long and probably busy day would have given us some clearer insight into what life meant and how it was faced in that particular part of Manitoba.

True, the subject-matter of Mr. Grove's essays jealously excludes human intrusion—unless as a point of harmonious picture interest in the landscape in *The Turn of the Year* —and this particular occasion could not very well have been made an exception. But the point is, this very exclusion of human interest is the characteristic of Mr. Grove's most personal books. Later, when we are reading his novels dealing with life in this Manitoba settlement, the remembrance of how unconsciously, how obliviously he turned his back on all human intercourse will be a help in explaining some of their limitations.

Again, we shall not have accompanied Mr. Grove very far until we discover how intensely absorbed he is in the transient natural phenomena taking place in the world about him. He seldom takes a sweeping view out towards the horizon. It is upon what is close beside him, what may be scrutinized with the greatest care and detail, that he likes to exercise his thought. He then searches to discover the truest word in which to pass his experience on to us. His description of hoar-frost-laden woods is an illustration, but too long to quote here in full. It begins:

Oh, the surprising beauty of it! There stood the trees, motionless under that veil of mist, and not their slenderest finger but was clothed in white. And the white it was! A translucent white, receding into itself, with strange backgrounds of white behind it—a modest white, and yet full of pride. An elusive white, and yet firm and substantial. The white of a diamond lying on snow-white velvet, the white of a diamond in diffused light. None of the sparkle and colour play that the most precious of stones assumes under a definite, limited light which proceeds from a definite, limited source. Its colour play was suggested, it is true, but so subdued that you hardly thought of naming or even recognizing its component parts. There was no red or yellow or blue or violet, but merely that which might flash into red and yellow and blue and violet, should perchance the sun break forth and monopolize the luminosity of the atmosphere. There was, as it were, a latent opalescence.

And every twig and every bough, every branch and every limb, every trunk and every crack even in the bark was furred with it. It seemed as if the hoar frost still continued to form. It looked heavy, and yet it was nearly without weight. Not a twig was bent down under its load, yet with the halo of frost it measured fully two inches across.

There are many accurate, delicate details recorded here: "It looked heavy, and yet it was nearly without weight. Not a twig was bent down under its load." And yet it is impossible to read such a length of lines without feeling the tendency to overdo which is latent in it. The virtuosity of such a passage, the calculation, the elaboration of such a delicate natural thing jars on one as the rhetorical repetition of the word "white" comes to do. It is the kind of picture which needs only one apt line or word of poetic insight to kindle the imagination of the reader to recreate it for himself. In *The Yoke of Life*, Mr. Grove himself has this sentence:

As the picture which he had seen decomposed itself into its elements, Len felt sorry with that sadness which overcomes us when we see or hear a beautiful marvel rationally explained.

Mr. Grove holds us wholly intent on a very narrow world, for it is only a limited field could come into such a scrutinizing ken. Still, all the time we feel there is at the back of his interest a deep realization of the vast universe which envelops us. We might take, for example, first his remarks on the "exfoliation" of the snow-drifts:

Strange to say, this very exfoliation gave it something of a quite peculiarly desolate aspect. It looked so harsh, so millennial-old, so antediluvian and pre-Adamic! I still remember with peculiar distinctness the slight dizziness that overcame me, the sinking feeling in my heart, the awe and the foreboding that I had challenged a force in nature which might defy all tireless effort and the most fearless heart.

Again, in "The Gloom of Summer," he has been describing the forest through which the road ran—its denseness, the loftiness of the trees, the tangle of underbrush, the swampy earth—when suddenly he turns aside thus:

Dark, unknown, gloomy, the shade of night seemed to crouch in these woods, ready to leap out on the clearings and the road, as soon as the sun should sink, threatening with incomprehensible potentialities. . . . I could not get rid of the feeling that they (these woods) were not a monument of the intensity of life so much as rather one of everlasting death itself.

Considering the trend of passages like these, the mysterious sense they disseminate that we are wrapped round by immeasurable and impenetrable elements of creation, and then remembering the determined interest in conditions immediately beside us in both time and space to which Mr. Grove holds us, it would seem as if we distinctly heard him command: "Occupy yourself with this, poor, helpless, puny human atom that you are, because it is all that is given you to know."

In his chapter "A Call for Speed" are a few sentences which throw light on this side of his thought. They begin:

Most serious minded men at my age, I believe, become profoundly impressed with the futility of "it all."

Again, in his poem "Science," he dwells on a slightly different aspect of the same idea. "Within a lightless cave," "a sightless eft," who, however, inherits from remote ancestors a knowledge of the sun, gropes and dreams and puzzles his exploring way. He succeeds in finding food for his body only, the longing of his breast is unfed. Further search is but torture, for it brings no light. Nothing within his world corresponds to his dream and wish and hope. Finally the poem ends with these lines:

> Such is, O God, man's high exalted state,
> The dignity with which he was endowed
> When he emerged from chaos inchoate,
> Erect, celestial-eyed, and astral-browed.
> Yet will he, God, go on and build his dream
> And in mute censure hold it up to Thee.
> Perhaps when he has perished, his frail scheme
> Will serve as model to new worlds to be.

If these lines speak Mr. Grove true, he looks upon life as something man must be "deluded into living on." Conrad has a phrase which from this point of view describes the armoured protection against life Mr. Grove reveals in his work: "The detached curiosity of a subtle mind, and the high tranquillity of a steeled heart."

But this is not the right note to leave sounding as these books of beautiful word pictures are closed. The rich, musical, polished prose tempts one to make many and long quotations. The whole series of evening, sunset, and twilight scenes called "The Harvest" might be quoted to show how we are allowed to see through a very artistic and cultured eye the full gorgeousness of hue and shade in earth and air and cloud. Then, as the climax on this sloping field, passing into the shadows of evening while yet the heavens are full of light, there come two black horses drawing a wagon with a hayrack and a single man. This man, his wagon, his team, etched against that golden west, make a picture Millet himself might have wrought. And Mr. Grove's method of depicting the man has not a little in common with that master's method. He shows him to us doing his work, lifting his sheaves with his fork and building his load with such a rightness of the worker's movements—of a practised good worker's movements—that all weight, all motion in the picture and the posture are most satisfyingly right. This scene ends as follows:

And when he picked up with his fork what he intended to lift, I could only marvel at his strength and skill. Slowly, without hurry, but also without waste of time, he would force the fork with its tremendous load up, with a steady exertion, till he held the handle high overhead; and then he would throw the sheaves off with the slightest of jerks so that they fell just where he wanted them. . . . His body seemed to shorten and to broaden when he did that; and never did I see a wrong move or a lost motion, never hurry, never delay.

Settlers of the Marsh, a novel, was Mr. Grove's next book. It has the same Manitoba district for its background, and a young Swede immigrant—a native country man—for its hero. Mr. Grove had thus material which he understood perfectly. The opening up of this novel leaves nothing to be desired. There is a rightness about the descriptions and a harmony between them and the undertone of mood and feeling. Mr. Grove introduces his hero, Niels Lindstedt, a strong, well-built, quiet chap, and his guide and friend Lars Nelson, in a natural way. They are pushing along from the end of rail to the farm on the edge of the bush, thirty miles distant, where they are to dig a well. The hard work and its deadening effect, which are to be emphasized in the life before them, are foreshadowed by this long tramp. And there is also foreshadowed that almost passive "stick-to-it-iveness" which will characterize their acceptance of New World conditions and summarize, in their limited view, the complete fulfilling of their own duty in the life of the community around them.

There is no forcing of the description of this walk, no heaping up of hardship. It is direct, and stamped by truth. They set out late in the afternoon, in the teeth of a cold November snowstorm. We enter fully with them into the steady uphill push against the north-west blast. As night fell and the trail drifted in, "the very ground under foot seemed to slide to the south-east." When alone on the road, lost and bewildered by the dark and the storm, "both would have liked to talk, to tell and to listen to stories of danger, of being lost, of hairbreadth escapes . . . but whenever one of them spoke, the wind snatched the word from his lips and threw it aloft." Such phrases of imaginative nicety add beauty to the truth.

The same naturalness marks an interesting account of their early days. Their thrifty progress, their schemes and dreams are convincingly set forth. There is a quiet, purposeful feeling of well-being and satisfaction with their lot, and what they are going to be able to do, which is characteristic of the serious-minded young working-man who sees his way clear to make and to save money. There is no bright, gay side, however, to these Swedes. There is no humour about them, no knocking of fun and a laugh out of the accidents of the day. There is nothing but their prosaic plodding and gathering of gear, each year a little ahead of the last, and all most gratifying to young men who have never known the thrill of possession before.

So far this circumscribed study is thoroughly well done, and written in a style exactly suited to it, quiet, simple, precise, and with besides an undertone of understanding sympathy running through it. But the author at length finds he must broaden out his hero's life, if his book is to be anything beyond a commentary on working conditions in a rather poor section of country. This is not easy because Niels, while attractive looking, energetic, and intelligent, is devoid of that interest which a copious outpouring of the gifts of the spirit or the intellect would give to him. To carry on his life successfully in the same vein, the author would require to be very familiar, one might almost say intuitively and lovingly familiar from childhood, with such prosaic surroundings and passive prosaic lives.

But this familiarity with the lives and thoughts of humdrum, ordinary, "low-brow" folk is what Mr. Grove's birth and training did not give him, and the interests and moods of the grown man could not cultivate. From this point of view he has written a little story, "Drama at the Crossroads," which throws a helpful light on him and his methods, as indeed do many passages of *Fruits of the Earth*, but it is not so easy to deal with them in brief space. "Drama at the Crossroads" gives an admirable insight into what takes the place of sympathetic understanding for him. It is a description of the various buyers and sellers at a small prairie shop of an Armenian Jew during the Saturday evening that his daughter eloped with a young farmer. The picture, as far as Mr. Grove makes it, is authentic beyond doubt, but the little glimpses given of himself are what interests us here.

In the early stages of the setting, the author has sauntered away some miles from the scene of action, "and squatted on the flank of the ridge looking out into the calm of the wilderness." "I sat for hours". Then, as he turns back, the passing of the Jew on his light wagon piled high with goods leads him to make this reflection:

Old Kalad, the fat, serious-minded grabber of the pennies of the pioneers that were hidden in the bush, had suddenly something heroic for me—like a conqueror who settles in the wilderness to fight its limits back.

Such was his frame of mind preparatory to getting into understanding fellowship with the prairie folk who would gather that evening.

Once back in the shop, he cannot make himself at home, he cannot drop into easy and familiar relations with any one. At one minute "not wishing to intrude," at another "in order not to disturb" . . . "I went back outside and roamed for hours." During that ramble he heard a laugh from the store, and felt "as if this world which lay spread out before me were not made for that laugh—this world with its moon and its stars, with the sigh of the woods, and the cool breath of the night."

However, "since the mosquitos were troublesome," he went in again and "drifted about listening." It is beyond doubt to such drifting times we owe the well-chosen descriptive phrases with which he often memorably delineates his men and women. Yet it is not a method to bring him understanding. His own words describing Ellen, in *Settlers of the Marsh*, give the result perfectly:

She gave a level, quiet look . . . it did not establish a bond, it held no message, neither of acceptance nor of disapproval . . . it was an undisguised, cool, disinterested scrutiny.

Having this key, we understand what Mr. Grove may see and what he will have to leave out. Against such scrutiny all human beings lock their breasts.

But to return to Niels now, with our added insight from the "Crossroads Drama." His creator has carried him along his prosaic way as far as he has knowledge of that type—he has depicted his working life. Now to broaden out his study he marries Niels, forges off on another trail, completely changes the tone of his book, alters with it the style of his writing, and the result is that the account of Niels's life ceases to ring true. It becomes incredible.

A film-picture-like succession of scenes tell of Niels's married life. They are written up in their more lurid moments by inverted, artificial captions like this: "On a silken bed, upstairs in the house, there lay a woman, it is true. . . ." This ends with Neils shooting his wife and spending six years in the penitentiary. He returns home then and marries Ellen, which was his foreordained fate from the earliest pages of the book. They then go and live the life they would have lived had the melodrama episode never entered—but Mr. Grove leaves that story to our own imagination. The educated, European Mr. Grove, accustomed from childhood to a different world, had a traveller's and an observer's trained eye for certain aspects of the new life about him on the prairies. But for fathoming the inner feelings of such people he had neither the long and instinctive insight gained by acquaintance with them from childhood to guide him, nor had he the natural interest to direct his observations deep enough in worlds outside his limits.

No doubt an author has a perfect right to demand that anything he wishes may happen in his story. Because an incident is preposterous, is no reason to exclude it. But equally just is the reader's demand that everything has to be credible, given the characters the author has chosen. Everything has to be made possible. And this is what Mr. Grove fails to do in his continuation of *Settlers of the Marsh*, and in his other novels once his own firsthand knowledge and the careful observations he made as an eye-witness come to an end.

How incredible is this situation: this young man Niels has for several years been a hardworking, ambitious, sensitive chap, forming his own ideals of home and spending himself generously to do his part in bringing them about. At the same time he has been cherishing in his heart his own simple, characteristic romance. Again, he has been delineated as an alert, wide-awake young workman, who has good natural ability—he mastered English easily by spending a winter in the neighbouring town. It has been pointed out how much his insight and understanding have been increased by the fact that he has migrated and adapted himself to a new land. Yet this is the man we are to believe married the notorious woman of the settlement, Mrs. Vogel, who had been known to him since his first Sunday there. Even more, she had been his nearest neighbour, only two miles distant, and Bobby the fifteen-year-old, who worked with him and is represented as of quite secondary general intelligence to Niels, understood fully all about her.

There is another serious and fundamental weakness in the romantic side of Mr. Grove's novels. It is this. Mr. Grove himself has, at heart, no interest in it. He tells us in his article "The Novel":

I abominate the common love story—the story of prenuptial love, almost as violently as I abhor the gramophone, the telephone, or the radio. In life both young men and young maids are peculiarly uninteresting at the time when they see each other as they are not.

For a reader who has read Mr. Grove's novels before reading this essay, coming on this sentence is like the old story of finding the letters *d o g* printed under the drawing of a dog. Again, in his essay on "Realism in Literature," he has two more sentences which might be linked to this first:

He (the author) . . . cannot convincingly represent a character or happening which finds no echo in himself, he delimits his work by his own personality. . . . He cannot reproduce except what was potentially in him.

With this feeling on the subject, he produced in *Settlers of the Marsh* the unreal, sensational scenes between Niels and Mrs. Vogel, and the likewise unconvincing, wooden ones between Niels and Ellen. But poor Ellen is a lay figure always. She exists only in her author's eye. Let us take for example that scene where Niels and Ellen have had their lively, happy walk together across the country, around the school, and finally in fear of a thunderstorm take shelter by a straw stack. Ellen, moved by the onset of the storm or the presence of her lover, rushes to the top of the stack to welcome the wind. How does her creator picture her at this moment—a moment supreme in her relationship with Niels? Are we shown her in a way to bring this home to us? Do we see her face and her figure as her lover Niels would be scrutinizing them then to try to find out an answer to some of the silent, unspeakable questions which were thronging both his heart and hers? No. We see her instead as the pictorial artist, Mr. Grove, intent upon describing his storm, sees her. She becomes merely a fine point of interest in the centre of his wind-swept scene:

Up rises the girl in the storm, holding on to her bonnet with both her hands, leaning back into the wind, her skirt crackling and snapping and pulling at her strong limbs.

Thus the artist "delimits his work by his own personality."

If it is his artist's interest which comes between him and this scene between Niels and Ellen in his first novel, in his second, *Our Daily Bread*, it is his "abomination" of the subject which hurries him scornfully through the chapter named "The Leaven of Sex is at Work." Herein Mr. Grove accumulated all his courting and marrying, evidently on the principle that if a sufficient number of "peculiarly uninteresting young men and maids" were lumped to-gether and despatched wholesale, something "peculiarly interesting" might be the result—at any rate it would get the whole sorry lovesick business over with quickly for the august author. And so it did, but unfortunately it produced for the reader a similar indifferent, lordly con-tempt towards the eight puppets which were jerked into four pairs. So little attention did any one of them attract that beyond a query now and then about which side of his old father's *ego* was supposed to contribute to such a one his individual brand of practical, energetic competence, or of mean-souled selfishness, no one ever considered them. They were throughout personifications, sometimes vivid enough, but they were never flesh and blood.

But it is pleasant to turn from Mr. Grove's treatment of "pre-nuptial love" to his delineation of the old man's character in *Our Daily Bread*. It is a sharp turn. A turn from a theme abhorred to one doted upon, and the reader's interest mounts in accordance.

It is not that the old man's character is a pleasant one to follow. It is the very reverse. But it is that Mr. Grove has herein a problem he finds worth while, and therefore spreads it out before us with detailed, ambitious thoroughness and seriousness which make it not only impressive but often very human. Occasionally when taking his readers into his confidence, Mr. Grove tells them that he has a scent for tragedy, by which he frequently means for failure. And certainly anyone with a scent for failure would have a topic very much to his liking in *Our Daily Bread*. The protagonist, John Elliot, in the last score years of his life, reaps a sorry harvest after living what he conceived to be a life of serving God through all the previous years.

Mr. Grove's problem, then, is so to work out John Elliot's character that his destiny will be seen to have been bound up in it. He does this largely by showing the interplay of character between John Elliot and his ten children. In this study he is more happy in less ambitious, casual lines than in his larger dialogues and set scenes. Whenever lengthy conversation is indulged in, Mr. Grove's limits in the knowledge of human kind make it painfully unreal. In such pages we forget the characters and live with the author. Mrs. Elliot's talks with John and with Isabel before their approaching marriages illustrate this. But John Elliot's brief utterances and meditations, snapped out here and there, have a human, living ring. For example, he was out of sorts with all his children, and then received news that Henrietta had a baby girl and called her Juanita. One can distinctly hear the peevish old man's, "A girl? Juanita? How was that pronounced?"

We also follow John Elliot, quite naturally, considering his years, through much illness and many deaths. And yet, there are so many such scenes, with unpleasant sickroom details sprinkled about so generously that the novel, with nothing to counteract and soften the effect, takes on a morbid atmosphere. Besides, all this accumulation of disease throws so little additional light on old John. He revealed himself once for all in the face of such trials when he received the news of his youngest son's death. In one brief paragraph his creator bares for us his puny heart:

Arthur had died in action. It affected his father strongly. Not that he mourned greatly; he had hardly known the boy; but the first of his children had died! How long did he himself have to live?

Death itself can call forth no warm, loving, unselfish cry from John Elliot. Nothing but a futile little worrying question as to the number of his own days left.

The futility of it all was that in spite of the seemingly endless series of family meetings and of family shiftings, the old man's eyes were never opened to see what a broad, generous, beautiful, unselfish life his might have been, and that he had missed it by his own pettiness. Had he ever caught a glimpse of this rich might-have-been while fumbling along in his ugly present, then the dreary tale of his days would have had significance. John Elliot would have developed soul. As it is, his unavailing old age and final collapse dull the force of the picture. The reader, like his children, has lost interest in him before his end. He is not great enough, he has too meagre an endowment of heart and spirit and intellect for his fate to move one as tragic. A tragedy demands a noble man defeated by ignoble circumstances, whereas John Elliot was a selfish man betrayed by his own selfishness.

It is not necessary to treat at length the third novel, *The Yoke of Life*. It is largely working over the same ground and garnering a poorer crop. Len, the chief figure, has his setting in a regular Grovian family. His childhood is spent in trembling fear of his father and pitying services to his mother, and emphatically the best chapter in the book—indeed the best chapter in all Mr. Grove's novel writing —is the opening one where this is disclosed. In these first pages, Mr. Grove proves that he has an eye so sharp to observe personal traits that it is wholly lack of interest in matters not central to his own serious concerns which prevents his character drawing always attaining this height.

Len as a worker lives in the same prairie land vacuum in which we met Niels. Did space permit, it would be a fruitful study to compare many passages in *The Yoke of Life* with similar ones from other books. However, one will have to suffice. Take for example the poker game at the camp, and place it beside the game in the bunk-house at MacKenzie's in *A Search for America*. In the bunk-house there is a feeling of reality about the scene. The atmosphere is tense and silent, and the men are alive. In *The Yoke of Life* there is but stagey and melodramatic conversation and atmosphere. Yet it is in basis the same scene. But one convinces; it is given at first hand, with natural narrative. The other is second hand; it is a composite picture made up of various reminiscences and retouches, and put together in such proportions that the life has been dropped out.

Unlike *Our Daily Bread*, a large part of this third novel is concerned with the story of "pre-nuptial love," and again the author's violent abhorrence of his topic brings it to grief. Len as a lover, to borrow the words from his sweetheart's thoughts, is "so ponderous, far-fetched, round-about," and develops into such a self-centred, selfish cad that it is never possible to accept the idea that he loved Lydia, or indeed to accept him with Lydia at all. So far removed from credible character drawing are Len and Lydia that a reader thinks of them only as some kind of a footnote exercise to illustrate the opinions on proper endings for novels or on realism in literature expressed by

Mr. Grove in *It Needs to be Said*. The foundation for their existence has been evolved out of theories, and in no scene does it hold the reader as a page of life and truth.

There is new material to be found, however, in Len the student. Our author has taught boys, and understands how intelligent, sensitive youngsters will rise to a loved teacher's words. In connection with this, the teacher explains to Len his life:

So I became a teacher and worked up in that line. Not because I wanted to make more money, but because I hungered and thirsted after a higher and truer idea of life. That hunger and thirst itself is happiness, Len. We shall never still it. We shall never find truth. But we must strive after it without standing still.

In the undertone here sounds the characteristic message Mr. Grove has for schoolboys old and young. Another expression of it is found in one of the polished musical paragraphs of *Over Prairie Trails*:

I have lived in southern countries, and I have travelled rather far for a single lifetime. Like an epic, stretch my memories into dim and ever receding pasts. I have drunk full and deep from the cup of creation. The Southern Cross is no strange sight to my eyes. I have slept in the desert close to my horse, and I have walked in Lebanon. I have cruised in the seven seas and seen the white marvels of ancient cities reflected in the wave of incredible blueness. But then I was young. When the years began to pile up, I longed to stake off my horizons, to flatten out my views. I wanted the simpler, the more elemental things, things cosmic in their association, nearer to the beginning or end of creation. The parrot that flashed through "nutmeg groves" did not hold out so much allurement as the simple grey-and-slaty junco. The things that are unobtrusive and differentiated by shadings only—grey in grey above all—like our northern woods, like our sparrows, our wolves—they held a more compelling attraction than orgies of colour and screams of sound. So I came home to the

north. On days like this, however, I should like once more
to fly out and see the tireless wave and the unconquerable
rock. But I should like to see them from afar and dimly
only—as Moses saw the promised land. Or I should like to
point them out to a younger soul, and remark upon the
futility and innate vanity of things.

This quotation also affords a very good example of both
the most significant and the least significant aspects of his
work. It gives an insight into his unusual temperamental
nature; it discloses his wide and varied travelling, his
cosmopolitan learning, and his elusive aspirations; and it
emphasizes his refined artist's eye, and his solitary brooding
temper; and yet it reveals with all his learning an empty-
handed gleaning of any satisfying philosophy of life.

Considering such extracts, one wonders if Mr. Grove
would be a good guide for that "younger soul." Should we
not rather leave our children full of the gladness of the
world, and not introduce them to its vanities and its sor-
rows? These will break upon the growing life all too
soon. The constant ideal of the glory will be the best
antidote in the end to meet the inevitable gloom.

Mr. Grove's next study, *Fruits of the Earth*, seemingly
attempts, as did *Our Daily Bread*, to carry on the pedestrian everyday life of a prairie farmer throughout his
maturity—the very material, therefore, he shied away from
in *Settlers of the Marsh*. As the European-trained Mr.
Grove sees this life, it discloses no beauty and no grace, as
it would, for instance, to Laura Salverson, steeped from
childhood in its sentiment, beauty, and affection. Her
page would have both laughter and tears. Nor does this
academic man understand the very simple unsophisticated
rural Manitoba community. But this has been pointed out
before.

However, it is not as fiction or a novel Mr. Grove himself intended this book. He considers it as a sort of
fictionized economic history of the district. In that light, it
would not be very valuable for a research student of the

future, who would require a great many more facts and figures to base his own conclusions upon. It thus unfortunately falls between two stools. It is not a novel and it is not history. And moreover it is written in the most pedestrian, unimaginative narrative style of all his books. To use his own adjectives applied to the settlers, his whole chronicle might be called "slow, deliberate, earthbound." So it happens his readers are prone to cry out, like the author himself when overcome by the northern grey: "On days like this, however, I should like once more to fly out and see the tireless wave and the unconquerable rock."

But the book which has been kept for the last, *A Search for America*, is one that has a dramatic lifelike variety which does not pall. It is a unique *Pilgrim's Progress*, partly autobiographical, partly allegoric, showing how the author's outlook upon life became changed by the encounters he had with all sorts and conditions of men in the United States and Canada.

A brief epitome will make clear how this came about. As he was sailing up the St. Lawrence on his arrival, his ambition was "to found a home and an atmosphere for myself." "Cicero's *otium cum dignitate* was what I desired." But in the experience developed by one job after another and many days jobless, by menial service and shattered hopes and eye-opening by shocks, by earnings and lendings and losses, by the knowledge which came from helping hands and cheating hands, from kindly interest and from contempt, from sickness and pain, from tramping and watching and solitary communings under the stars, and particularly by "sedulous enquiry" day after day as to how the matter stood, there is gained for Frederick Philip Grove a priceless tuition in the ties linking a man to his fellows. Henceforth his demands from life for himself were supplemented by feelings of necessity for sympathy and responsibility towards his fellowmen. And dutifully did he try not to slur over this lesson. But it was a hard saying for the born student, for the fastidious classic scholar, for the aloof solitary tramp who writes explicitly and implicitly on every page, "I love nature more than man."

The result was that there were from now on two Mr. Groves, and they are never wholly reconciled to each other. There is first the self-disciplined Mr. Grove, the teacher, the champion, the counsellor, and the guide of his less able fellow-immigrants. So earnest has he been about this that for some thirty years it has been one of the chief factors determining his habitation and avocation.

And secondly there is the European-trained Mr. Grove —the cultured, widely-read student, the sensitive artist, sufficient unto himself, yet eager in himself to create in literature what he confidently feels he can do and what, when done, will be of value to his fellowmen. He is an accurate and delicate observer within the limits of his academic interests, and a pondering philosopher, who, however, often contents himself, in this field, with inexplicit words which he would cast aside impatiently as most inadequate were he in his role of observer trying to catch some transient phase of a fog or mist or other natural phenomenon. This man wishes to be solitary and laborious. He would follow cheerfully Emerson's command: "Go cherish your soul; expel companions; set your habits to a life of solitude." And likewise would he believe the promise:

Then will the faculties rise fair and full within, like forest trees and wild flowers; you will have results which when you meet your fellowmen you can communicate, and they will gladly receive.

And, moreover, this Mr. Grove has not left behind him in Europe the scholarly ambitions of his youth. He is quite fully prepared to aim as high as Emerson demanded:

The public can get public experience, but they wish the scholar to replace to them these private, sincere, divine experiences of which they have been defrauded by dwelling in the street. It is the noble, manlike, just thought which is the superiority demanded of you, and not crowds but solitude confers this elevation.

"It is the noble, manlike, just thought which is the superiority demanded of you." In the patient, thorough finish of his workmanship, in the fastidious rightness and accuracy of his words, phrases, and descriptions, in the sensitive recording and discriminating of the delicately shaded moods of a solitary man, Mr. Grove has given us an example and set a standard of superiority which even to himself—his own best critic and his own best guide— must give great artistic satisfaction.

Again, if we consider his intentions, his aims, the kind of work he strives to do and the significance of his chosen subject matter, the words "noble" and "manlike" may indeed be applied. Truth is the aim and interest of his art. But each of us sees truth through the haze of his own temperament. And for Mr. Grove, ever baffled by the two sides of his own being, the finest content he can put into his writing is that all experience is full of the sighing of the prisoner of the soul who finds no respite in perpetually seeking for the never found. There is none but his own seeking. As the teacher said to Len, "That hunger and thirst itself is happiness. We shall never still it."

His Canadian readers appreciate Mr. Grove's merits very highly, as witness the unquestioned position they assign him in their literary world. But one thing is clear. His books have limitations, and have been ranked according to them. Haphazard as these preferences may seem to the author computing the time and labour which went to the making of his various works, yet they are based on inherent characteristics. *A Search for America*, *Over Prairie Trails*, and *The Turn of the Year*, together with certain chapters from his novels, compose the favourite list. His Canadian public will always welcome, read, cherish, even buy—and perchance beg, borrow and lend —such books as these.

GROVE'S TRAGIC VISION

DESMOND PACEY

"A work of literature," Grove declared in *It Needs to be Said*, "is a work of art exactly to that extent to which it disengages the generally tragic reaction of the human soul to the fundamental conditions of man's life on earth." By this standard, he is certainly successful himself. The vision of human experience which is conveyed through his novels is an intensely tragic one. Life to Grove is a perpetual struggle, a struggle of man to assert his will against the various pressures of his environment:

Life swarms with conflict. We might almost go so far as to says that life *is* conflict. Conflicts, in the concrete, are of such exceedingly common occurrence that, in observing life, one is reminded of a sea in a storm where all large waves—great issues—are beset with smaller waves—the minor conflicts—the backs of which in turn are rippled by the wind—these ripples representing the quarrels and squabbles of menial minds. If life is not essentially of the stuff of conflicts, it tends at least to break up into a series of continual conflicts.

To this tragic vision Grove has given concrete embodiment in his novels. The action of each of them consists of "a series of continual conflicts." Struggling to escape from the net of circumstances, his characters either become more intricately involved in it or become entangled in another net. Each of his central characters has a dream of future fulfilment, and for each the result is frustration. John Elliot dreams of living in the patriarchal manner with his children comfortably established on farms around him; he dies at last alone, his children scattered, his own home ruined and deserted. Len Sterner dreams of becoming a great scholar, the master of all knowledge; he

From *Frederick Philip Grove* by Desmond Pacey (Toronto: Ryerson, 1944), 123-134.

dies sordidly, a victim of forces beyond his control. The same general pattern is traced in each of the novels.

The sources of this pervasive frustration are many. Basic is the perpetual conflict between man and his natural environment. Like Hardy, Grove oscillates between conceptions of a universe controlled by forces deliberately malignant towards man and one controlled by forces which are simply ignorant of or indifferent to human aspirations. But that these forces override man's will and thwart his purposes he is in no doubt. Here are some typical sentences from his novels:

I felt as if I were in the hands of powers beyond my own or any human control; as if the gods were grinding me into their grist and grinding me exceedingly small.

There seemed to be some external power which shuffled men about as you shuffle a deck of cards.

Life had him in its grip and played with him; the vastness of the spaces looked calmly on.

He was a leaf borne along in the wind, a prey to things beyond his control, a fragment swept away by torrents.

This sense of the interplay of vast inscrutable forces beyond the knowledge or control of man permeates all of his work. It is in part responsible for that quality of universality which his novels possess; for we have the sense that we are witnessing not merely the fate of individuals but of the whole human race.

This view of man's conduct as determined by forces external to him is of course a common one in the literature of the late nineteenth and early twentieth centuries: one thinks of Zola, Hardy and Dreiser, to name but three. But Grove's conception of these forces, although undoubtedly the result of the same *Zeitgeist* as produced the similar views of the writers mentioned, resembles rather the Greek conception of Fate than the scientific determinism of the naturalists. He makes no mention of the heredity of his characters as a shaping force in their conduct, as does Zola in *Les Rougon-Macquart* and Hardy in *Tess of the D'Urbervilles*, nor of the moulding power of early environment. Indeed, in *It Needs to be Said*, he expressly attacks the scientific pretensions of the naturalistic school of fiction, holding that art should not rely upon the ephemeral conclusions of science.

If Grove is thus somewhat vague regarding the nature of the forces which control our lives, he is clear enough in portraying the concrete examples of the opposition between man and his surroundings. Wind, hail, drought and dust continually assail his characters. Storms play a prominent part in all his novels, and into his accounts of them he introduces a quality of deliberate malignity. A blizzard is described as "a merciless force which was slowly numbing them by ceaseless pounding." The pioneers toil for months to produce a promising crop; hail wipes it out in a few seconds.

Even where man succeeds in gaining some kind of temporary control over his environment, there is still the less spectacular but no less deadly enmity of Time to contend with. Abe Spalding, by dint of heroic effort, withstands the power of storm and flood, but his energies and his creations are being gradually consumed by the devouring years. As has been pointed out, some of the most expressive passages in Grove's books are those in which he draws upon his knowledge of archaeology to set man's temporary triumphs in the context of eternity.

But his conception of life as a matter of perpetual conflict embraces more than the struggle between man and the forces of Fate, Nature and Time outside him. Man must also contend with his fellows and with himself. The relationships between people in his novels are never easy, always tense. There is the conflict between the generations, one of his favourite themes. John Elliot, Abe

Spalding, Ralph Patterson, Mack Kolm—each of them wrestles with the wills of his children, seeking to dominate them and ultimately failing. As Grove puts it in *It Needs to be Said*: "The eternal conflict between parents and children results always in some sort of tragedy. If the children are vitally stronger, the tragedy is that of the parents; if the parents are vitally stronger, the tragedy is that of the children." And within each generation, in turn, are tragic conflicts of will. Between brothers and sisters there are jealousies, suspicions, colliding desires. Most agonizing of all, there is the conflict of sex.

Agonizing, for in Grove's novels sex is a source of far more agony than ecstasy. It would probably not be an exaggeration to say that there is not a single satisfying sexual relationship in all of his work. Sex to Grove—he uses the phrase himself, in *The Yoke of Life*—is a curse. In *Settlers of the Marsh* Niels Lindstedt is torn between the neurotically lustful Clara and the neurotically inhibited Ellen, and in the background is the terrible story of the sexual relationship of Ellen's parents; in *Our Daily Bread* there is Mrs. Elliot's horrible deathbed sense of guilt regarding her marital relations, and the frustration of Henrietta and Pete; in *The Yoke of Life* we witness the tragic outcome of Len's irresistible desire for the faithless Lydia; in *Fruits of the Earth* there is the gradual deterioration of Abe's marriage, and the seduction of his daughter; in *Two Generations* there is Ralph's sexual frustration, Alice's attraction to her brother, Nancy's adultery, Cathleen's excessive sexual demands. Either his characters are inhibited, burdened with a sense of guilt or shame which renders physical intimacy revolting, or they are excessively lustful and even lecherous. In his autobiography, Grove offers an explanation of his treatment of sex:

For the purposes of the pioneer conquest of nature certain qualities are needed, in man, which are incompatible with that tender devotion which alone can turn the relations of the sexes into a thing of beauty. Untamed land is a hard taskmaster; but, as a rule, the task is tackled only by men who are fit for it and, therefore, more or less unfit for that other task of sublimating physical needs into the iridescent play of desire and satisfaction which characterizes the sexual relation in more "advanced," more "sophisticated" civilizations. When, in the man, the gift for idealization and sublimation is not more or less absent under pioneer conditions, the fact usually leads to disaster of some kind; and I believe that in my books, grim as they may seem, I have made room for that tragedy too.

That may be a true account of the nature of sex in pioneer life, but it is not a complete explanation of Grove's handling of sex in his novels. It ignores the fact that when he treats of other environments and other people, his view of sex remains the same: neither Nancy nor Cathleen, of *Two Generations*, are pioneers. It also ignores the fact that Grove seldom represents the men as being primarily to blame for sexual aberration and suffering. The brunt of the responsibility usually rests on the women. It is Clara who leads Niels astray, Lydia who is faithless to Len, Nancy who betrays George.

Whatever the explanation of Grove's treatment of sex, it certainly accords well with his general vision of life and thus tends positively towards the integration of his work. Tribute must also be paid to him for his frankness. He has had the courage to treat the subject more frankly than any other Canadian writer—and in the face of our continuing puritanism it demanded courage. In spite of his frankness —or, rather, because of it—there is nothing approaching the obscene. He never leers or smirks, nor attempts in any way to titillate the senses. Very rarely does he even touch upon the physical aspects of sex; it is the anguish of sexual desire and frustration which is his primary concern. Indeed, if one were to criticize Grove's treatment of sex it would not be at all in the way that the puritans criticize him. The charge would rather be that he does not give sex its due, that he tends to leave us with the impression that he would prefer that it did not exist.

This matter of sex bridges the two final forms of conflict in Grove's novels. It is a conflict between one person and another; it is a conflict within the person himself. Man's intelligence and conscious will point in one direction, his deeper instincts in another. One thinks of Len Sterner, torn between his vision of an education and his consuming desire for Lydia; or of Niels Lindstedt, tortured by his craving for a woman whom his intelligence despises. It is significant that in both these cases, and others which might be mentioned, it is the non-rational forces which triumph. Over and over again in his novels Grove raises the question of whether we are free to make rational choices between alternative modes of behaviour, or are the predetermined products of our own temperament. His answer is always that we are what we are and can be no other.

His vision of a world in continuous conflict carries over into Grove's consideration of society. When, in *It Needs to be Said,* he discusses the nature of Canadian culture, he conceives it in terms of a conflict between the European and the American tradition, between cultural values on the one hand and material values on the other. The same is true of his vision of American civilization in *A Search for America*: it is the emerging product of a struggle between the Lincolns and the "con men," between honest idealism and graft. Perhaps the clearest example of all is provided by *The Master of the Mill,* where there are the conflicts between masters and men, between the masters themselves, between men and the machines.

But if tragic conflict is at the heart of Grove's view of life, he does not make the mistake, in Henry James' phrase, of failing to show also, in its place, the opposition, the escape. He supplements his negative account of man's prevailing tragic lot with the portrayal of positive human values. The final effect of his work is not dispiriting, for even in defeat his characters have the grandeur of heroism. They never submit tamely to the forces which seek their destruction. Our values may have no recognition or validity in the total framework of Space and Time, but they have validity for us in that they enable us to retain our sense of our own integrity.

Integrity—that is the supreme moral value to Grove, if I read his novels aright. That is the quality in his characters which wins for them our admiration: that whatever the obstacles, whatever the cost, they seek to adhere to their vision of the right. John Elliot, Abe Spalding, and the rest—their vision may be limited, partial, even false, but they cling fiercely to it, refusing to compromise or to turn back. The real failures in his novels are not these men, however grievously they may seem to fail, but the men who have no animating vision, who scatter their energies or go along with the prevailing current. He gives no supernatural sanction to this integrity. He does not suggest that the universe is ultimately moral, that the men who are true to their vision will earn an eternal reward. He does not echo the view of Browning, that a struggle for perfection in this world will lead to its realization in the next. The idea of a world beyond this never occurs. The only reward of integrity, in Grove's view, is the satisfaction of knowing we have clung to it.

But if enough men cling to it long and steadfastly enough, general progress will ensue. For Grove, in spite of the grimness of his vision, is not a blank pessimist. He rejects the evolutionary optimism of the Victorians, which held that progress would inevitably take place; but he does not rule out the idea of progress altogether. The conditions of life are harsh, the struggle intense, but there is prospect of amelioration. The first pioneer settlers often abandon their efforts to create a homestead, sometimes the efforts of four or five are necessary, but at last the wilderness is tamed. Perhaps his views in this regard are expressed most clearly, as they are most explicitly, in this passage from *A Search for America*:

We come indeed from Hell and climb to Heaven; the Golden Age stands at the never-attainable end of history, not at Man's origins. Every step forward is bound to be a compromise; right and wrong are inescapably mixed; the best we can hope for is to make right prevail more and more; to reduce wrong to a smaller and smaller fraction of the whole till it reaches a vanishing point.

Grove is reported to have said that the thing of first importance for a writer is that he chronicle "that reaction to life which is real and personal to him." So pervasive in Grove's own work is the reaction outlined in this chapter, so continuously and integrally woven into the texture of every book, that there is no question if its being a pose, a set of ideas adopted for effect. The steady uniformity of his vision gives to his work an organic unity of effect; its total bulk presents itself to us with a massive integrity.

But this reaction, it may be said, though personal to Grove, is not peculiar to him. It is a reaction widely shared in the contemporary world. That in no way impairs the value of his work, but it does suggest that his unique contribution does not lie there.

Grove's unique contribution to literature, I believe, is that he brought this philosophy to bear on the life of pioneer settlements. Others had expressed this philosophy, and others had treated the lives of pioneers in various parts of the world, but none had effected this peculiar combination. Peculiar, because a pioneer civilization, in the conventional view, is distinguished by attitudes quite different—freshness, vitality, buoyancy, exuberance, contempt for the old and traditional. Grove's philosophy, on the other hand, was born of a civilization conscious of its own imminent disintegration: of late nineteenth-century Europe, with its strained economic system, its religious doubt, its general perplexity and despair. Add to this general intellectual atmosphere the influence upon Grove of his archaeological training, and of Scandinavian fatalism whether inherited or acquired, and we have the sources of his outlook. This outlook, applied to the young civilization of the United States and particularly to that of the Canadian west, resulted in a new and distinctive portrayal of the pioneer effort.

Contrast, for example, Whitman's treatment of the pioneers with Grove's. In his poem, "Pioneers! O Pioneers!" Whitman speaks of them as "the youthful sinewy races" upon whom all the rest depend. He specifically detaches their destiny and prospects from that of the Old World:

Have the elder races halted?
Do they droop and end their lesson, wearied over there
    beyond the sea?
We take up the task eternal, and the burden and the
    lesson,
    Pioneers! O pioneers!
All the past we leave behind,
We debouch upon a newer, mightier world, varied world,
Fresh and strong the world we seize, world of labour and
    the march,
    Pioneers! O pioneers!

This note of confidence, of bravado, is quite alien to Grove's treatment. He does not despise the past, nor leave it out of consideration: he relates the endeavours of the pioneers to the endeavours of Man throughout the ages. He sees them not as a race apart, but simply as men confronting in a new environment the eternal and tragic conditions of man's life on earth. "And these things too shall pass away"—that is Grove's constant theme. The resultant effect is perhaps less immediately exciting than Whitman's, but it is more accurate and more profound. The buoyant optimism of the pioneers, the spectacular speed of their achievements, are largely mythical.

The two writers who are closest to Grove in their depiction of the pioneer life as one of struggle and frequent tragedy are also of Scandinavian origin: Knut Hamsun, author of *Growth of the Soil*, and Ole Rolvaag, author of *Giants in the Earth*. When Grove first read Hamsun's novel early in the twenties of this century, he at first felt that it made his own work unnecessary; but further consideration revealed that not to be the case. He thus describes the experience in his autobiography:

Hamsun's *Growth of the Soil* had recently appeared. Perhaps no other book has had a more decisive influence on the formulation of my theories. For the moment its effect on me was so great that I shelved my own book, *Pioneers*, unfinished. It seemed to me that Hamsun had done what I had attempted. It is characteristic of my whole attitude towards what I came to define to myself as art that I considered it entirely unnecessary to finish a book the subject of which had been successfully dealt with by another. This attitude is not invalidated by the fact that I resumed the book at a later stage. I came to the conclusion that my aim had, after all, been fundamentally different from Hamsun's. In Hamsun's book I came to see a thing I abhorred, namely romanticism; which means essentially a view of life in which circumstance is conquered by endeavour only if endeavour is aided by the *deus ex machina*. In other words, as I expressed it to myself, if man is justified by faith instead of by works; or if faith persists in the face of the strongest disproof and is ultimately upheld by an external intervention, natural or supernatural. This intervention is personified, in Hamsun's book, by the figure of Geissler. That has never been my view.

In other words, as Grove sees it (and I believe rightly) the point of difference between his own work and that of Hamsun is that his vision is more consistently realistic than that of the Norwegian novelist.

Between Grove and Rolvaag, the Norwegian-American novelist, the resemblance is even closer, though there seems to have been no contact of any kind between them. The resemblance is not merely one of art but of life. Both of Scandinavian origin, they were born within five years of one another, came to America in the last decade of the nineteenth century, settled finally in the new west, and wrote novels about prairie life. In certain respects, however, their lives differ considerably, and these differences go a long way to explain the differences in their art. Grove, as we have seen, came to America as a highly educated young man; Rolvaag came almost without schooling, though he had read a large number of romantic novels. Thus it is that although both record the life of the prairies realistically, stressing the difficulties and tragedies of the pioneer effort, Rolvaag's novels have not the philosophical depth of Grove's. Though *Giants in the Earth* is a great achievement, probably a greater single creation than any one of Grove's novels, it has not the power, as have Grove's best passages, to set the mind ranging over the whole story of human thought and history.

Grove retains, then, his distinctive place in literary history, achieved by the application to the life of a new area of a philosophy born of the long grim story of man's life on earth.

To decide on the truth or falsehood of this philosophy is not the business of a critic of fiction. It may be that his view of life is an unduly tragic one, that life contains more laughter and more joy than is suggested by his representation of it. But a novel, any work of art, is not like a pudding, contrived by adding ingredients in exact proportion. The value of art resides in its capacity to present for our contemplation a distinctive and challenging view of life. That Grove has such a distinctive attitude, that his studies of the life of a region set us pondering on the meaning of all life, is one of the chief sources of his power.

FREDERICK PHILIP GROVE AND THE CULTURE OF CANADA

B. K. SANDWELL

The career of Frederick Philip Grove is perhaps the most striking evidence that we have of the immaturity of Canadian culture. Born in 1871, to wealthy but incompatible parents in Sweden, he landed penniless and an orphan in Canada in 1893, and from then until 1912 he lived the life of a manual laborer and practically of a hobo in the American and Canadian west. Of the first forty years of his life, one half had been devoted to the acquisition of a very rich and wide-ranging education in various European universities, and to extensive travel in many parts of the world; the other half had been lived in the closest contact with the soil and with the life of the great generality of North American people. There could hardly have been a better preparation for a literary career of the most important kind.

But the value of this preparation was greatly reduced by an unfortunate condition in North American life around the turn of the century. Incredible as it may appear, this man of first-rate European culture, devoted to literature and constantly spending his spare time in the effort to produce a worthwhile book, managed to live for twenty years in the prairie provinces and adjacent States without ever meeting anybody who would tell him even the elementary facts that a book manuscript must in these days be typed and written on one side of the paper only. He was of course shy, and a foreigner, although he spoke perfect English; but for these two qualities he might have had better luck. But the fact remains that between 1893 and 1913 Grove was living the kind of life out of which the material for great literature most naturally grows, while the people who were producing literature

From *Saturday Night*, LXI (Nov. 24, 1945), 18. By permission of *Saturday Night*.

were themselves living on the other side of an impassable barrier.

The history of those twenty years of Grove's life seems to me to be a devastating comment upon the character of Canadian society, with its barriers between the immigrant and the older resident, between the manual worker and the clean-handed classes, between the people who think that they themselves matter and the other people who think they don't matter. It is a life the outline of which has long been known to students of Canadian literature, and the details of which are now admirably set forth in the volume *Frederick Philip Grove* by Desmond Pacey.

The slightest contact between Grove and other serious literary workers could not have failed to relieve his work of some of the qualities which have made it difficult of comprehension and appreciation for the great majority of readers. Nor would there have been the slightest danger that such contact would have impaired the intensely sincere and personal quality of his thinking. A man who went on writing, always in the hope of eventual publication, for thirty years before a single word appeared in print in a book was not the kind of man to be weakened or compromised by association with other literary workers. But the writer cannot do his best work in a vacuum: he derives enormous instruction from the reactions of his readers, and for thirty years, until his style was set and his structural method solidified, Grove went on writing without any readers, without any criticism, without even the experience of seeing his own words on the printed page. Many defects which a public reaction would almost unquestionably have remedied are still to be found in his writing, and still impede the popularity of his work.

Canadian culture did another injustice to Grove, and dropped another boulder in the path of Canadian literary progress, when it decided that his first full-length novel, *Settlers of the Marsh*, was obscene. "The reviewers," says

Dr. Pacey, "fumed at its indecency, radio speakers mournfully deplored its alleged filth, and most libraries banned it." It need hardly be said that these reactions were those of a juvenile community unaccustomed to the frank treatment of certain important aspects of life; the same reactions in a lesser degree followed the books of Canada's other serious novelist, Morley Callaghan. Mr. Callaghan was more immune to them because he had a large United States following, since his stories, though they actually deal with life on the north side of the St. Lawrence-Great Lakes waterway, are written in such a manner that the American reader can easily interpret them as dealing with the south side. Grove's milieu is frankly Canadian, and he has probably alienated much possible American sympathy by his outspoken declaration that he considers the United States to have abandoned its ideals and regards Canada as a much better example of true Americanism.

In spite of his deficiencies of style and structure—which I am convinced could have been greatly lessened by literary contacts during his period of isolation—Grove is by far the greatest philosophical literary artist to emerge as yet in Canada. He has been a profound student of the main currents of life in the great central prairies of this continent for fifty years—not the life of the urban population or of the intelligentsia, which is much the same in all parts of the continent, but the life of the masses of the people who are close to the soil, beaten upon by the storm and shone upon by the sun. Dr. Pacey makes the valid point that his work is closely akin to that of two other writers of Scandinavian origin, Knut Hamsun (unpopular at the moment for his fascist sympathies, which Grove would certainly not share) and Ole Rolvaag, author of *Giants in the Earth*.

His subject is the ancient subject of all tragedy, the conflict between the individual man and the forces of destiny which frustrate his efforts. The hero is to Grove the man who maintains his integrity of character in spite of this frustration, who clings to his vision and refuses to compromise or turn back. . . . In a country whose literature so far has been almost entirely concerned with the purely aesthetic values of nature and with the moral values which are associated with good bank credit, a novelist like Frederick Philip Grove is urgently needed.

It would not be fair to end this article without a word of tribute to the Canadian publishers who, with very limited prospects of profit to themselves, have done their full share towards putting his work before the public. The first firm to undertake a volume of his was McClelland & Stewart, and without their intervention he might have remained unheard of for another twenty years. The volume which they published (a collection of sketches) was however slightly less of a daring adventure than that of *Settlers of the Marsh* which Ryerson Press fathered owing to the discernment and faith of Dr. Lorne Pierce; and the Macmillan Company subsequently gave their imprint to several of the novels, probably owing to similar qualities in the late Hugh Eayrs. In the early stages of his advance towards publication, Grove owed much to two educationalists then prominent in the West, Arthur L. Phelps and Watson Kirkconnell. The difficulties which he experienced cannot be blamed on any individual: they are the direct results of the general cultural condition of Canada in the early years of the twentieth ("Canada's") century.

SPOKESMAN OF A RACE?

E. A. MCCOURT

Among Western writers Frederick Philip Grove seems to have seen more clearly than any other the responsibility of the writer who would give artistic expression to a distinctive regional spirit. He at least never minimized the

---

From *The Canadian West in Fiction* by E. A. McCourt (Toronto: The Ryerson Press, 1949), 56-70.

magnitude of the task nor the probability of failure. In his autobiography, *In Search of Myself*, he recalls a self-evaluation made in 1912 when he paused for a moment at middle age to ponder what he might do in the future:

Meanwhile there was, in this casting-up of accounts, one thing which stood on the asset side, against much which I must necessarily put down in the list of liabilities. The one asset consisted in this: that I could truthfully call my knowledge of the pioneering section of the west of the North American continent unique. At a glance I could survey the prairie country from Kansas to Saskatchewan or Alberta; and at a thought I could evaluate, in my own way of course, the implications of pioneer life. I, the cosmopolitan, had fitted myself to be the spokesman of a race—not necessarily a race in the ethnographic sense; in fact, not at all in that sense; rather in the sense of a stratum of society which cross-sectioned all races, consisting of those who, in no matter what climate, at no matter what time, feel the impulse of starting anew, from the ground up, to fashion a new world which might serve as the breeding place of a civilization to come. These people, the pioneers, reaffirmed me in my conception of what often takes the form of a tragic experience; the age-old conflict between human desire and the stubborn resistance of nature. Order must arise out of chaos; the wilderness must be tamed. No matter where I looked, then as today, I failed to see that the task of recording that struggle with nature had ever adequately been done, not even by Hamsun, who, for the sake of a pleasant ending, gave, to Isaak, Geissler. To record that struggle seemed to be my task. Perhaps, very likely even, I was foredoomed to failure in my endeavour; in fact, I seemed to see even then that I was bound to fail; but the attempt had to be made.

The premonition of failure here suggested was not the consequence of ordinary lack of confidence. Grove never underestimated his own powers. Indeed it is a serious weakness in him that he never seems to have been aware of the uncertainties of technique which mar much of his work and which humble self-appraisal might have done something to remedy. Rather, he felt that the petty necessity of earning his bread and butter prevented him from achieving the detachment which the great artist must have if he is to preserve his spiritual integrity:

In the last analysis it all came down to an economic problem. In order to see things once more from the outside, I must regain my distance; in order to regain my distance I must, economically and otherwise, get away from my present milieu.

But Grove was never permitted to escape from his "present milieu." It was his fate to be harassed all his life by the grimmest kind of economic necessity. None the less, the attempt to record adequately the "age-old conflict between human desire and the stubborn resistance of nature" was made. That attempt, as Grove had anticipated, failed. But the causes of failure lie not so much in the physical circumstances surrounding the act of creation, as Grove himself seems inclined to believe, as in his incomplete understanding of men and women.

Grove's story of man's struggle against the stubborn resistance of nature is localized in a Western Canadian setting in four of his novels: *Settlers of the Marsh* (1925), *Our Daily Bread* (1928), *The Yoke of Life* (1930) and *Fruits of the Earth* (1933). These four novels, published when Grove was well past middle age, together with two collections of descriptive essays, *Over Prairie Trails* (1922) and *The Turn of the Year* (1923), constitute the most considerable attempt yet made to describe the Western Canadian scene and to chronicle the lives of the people living within its borders. But in spite of Grove's avowed purpose, in none of the four novels is "the age-old conflict between human desire and the stubborn resistance of nature" the real centre of interest. John Elliot of *Our Daily Bread* and Abe Spalding of *Fruits of the Earth* are both resolute men who dream of owning vast tracts of land, not so much for the wealth inherent in possession as for the satisfaction of an obscure desire for power and permanency. The will to take roots is strong in both John Elliot and Abe Spalding, as it is in most men. The land itself, rather than its fruits, is what matters. But the struggle of the hero to conquer the land is not of paramount interest in either novel; the real battle is that of man against man, warfare that is never openly declared and which is really a clash between naturally conflicting rather than deliberately hostile forces. Such a struggle is inherently far more dramatic than one between man and his physical environment, as Grove clearly realized. Thus it is that in *Our Daily Bread* John Elliot's fight to establish himself as a wealthy landowner is over before the story which Grove has to tell begins. When we meet Elliot in the opening pages he is fifty-five years old; and the story of his conquest of the land is told in a paragraph. In *Fruits of the Earth* the hero, Abe Spalding, begins, it is true, frrom scratch; but it is obvious after the first few pages that he is destined to succeed in a material way; and the reader has at no time the feeling that he is witnessing a conflict of which the outcome is doubtful; indeed, he is almost certain to be bored by the repetitious examples of Abe's shrewdness and foresight. The struggle of man, personified in Abe Spalding, against nature, is easy, the outcome certain, and hence the dramatic interest inconsequential.

It is possible that had Grove concentrated to a greater degree than he did on the struggle of man to conquer nature—and this after all was his declared theme—his work might have been better than it is. But he was diverted into writing of a struggle even more dramatic—that between a man and his own flesh and blood—but for which he had limited talent. It is of course a kind of conflict which may be related to the struggle between man and his physical environment, since it is a natural development of that transitional stage of pioneer life when old and new inevitably clash; but Grove's knowledge of human nature was not, unfortunately, as broad or as deep as his knowledge of physical environment.

The conflict in both *Our Daily Bread* and *Fruits of the Earth* is as old as the race—man against his own flesh and blood, the father against his children. John Elliot and Abe Spalding are patriarchal types, anachronisms in their time, but the great agricultural and pastoral regions of the earth have always fostered the patriarchal way of life. To John Elliot it is a sin against nature that children should grow away from their parents and seek to lead independent lives; and the fact that his own children seek to escape his authority, and eventually do so, is the tragedy that darkens his declining years. In the same way Abe Spalding is concerned because his children grow away from him and the farm, attracted by the tawdry glitter of small-town life. But Abe is a stronger man than John Elliot, and a good deal less sensitive and introspective. In the end he reasserts a measure of authority over family and community and so gains a victory in which neither he nor the reader can take much pleasure.

Grove's failure is not one of judgment. The conflict between father and child is a magnificent theme of tragedy admitting of endless variation; but Grove is unable to make us feel that the situation as he describes it *is* tragic. John Elliot more often than not appears to be a selfish man of few inner resources whose desire to dominate his family removes him from the range of the reader's sympathy; hence in defeat he is not a tragic but merely a pathetic figure. Nor is it possible to feel much concern about the fate of the rebellious children, who are so devoid of life as to be incapable of arousing in the reader emotions of love or hate or even of interest. The Elliots are a large family; but the members are without discernible individuality.

It is unfortunate that Grove was unable to create characters capable of sustaining his theme, because his conception of the theme itself is a noble one. The conception is embodied in a passage which expresses John Elliot's attitude towards his life on the land, and towards his children who deny the validity of that attitude:

Through all his activities, then, a single purpose had run: the purpose of honourably raising his family, a large family at that. His favourite story from the Bible had been that of Abraham and his house; often had he repeated to himself the lines, "In blessing I will bless thee; and in multiplying I will multiply thy seed as the stars of the heaven and as the sand which is upon the sea-shore. And in thy seed shall all the nations of the earth be blessed."

Never had he, in these lines, seen or sought for evidences of verbal revelation; purely theological thought had been unknown to him. He had taken them simply as an expression of the marvel of fruitful propagation.

That single purpose had co-ordinated all things for him, had justified them; had seemed to transform his whole life with all its ramifications into a single, organic whole with a clear and unmistakable meaning. In that purpose he and his wife had been one; and so they had been fruitful and multiplied. It was the children's duty to conform, to become like them; and therefore, to obey them in all things, so as to multiply the seed themselves one day; so as not to let the strand thus created perish. To live honourably, to till the land, and to hand on life from generation to generation; that was man's duty; that, to him, in spite of all doubts, had meant and still meant serving God. Doubt had existed only as to details; it had never gnawed at the root of the fundamentals. . . .

Empires rose and fell; kings and high priests strove with each other; wars were fought; ripples on the sea of life. Underneath, deep down, that life itself went on as it had done in Abraham's time: the land was tilled to grow our daily bread. And this life, the life of the vast majority of men on earth, was the essential life of all mankind. The city with its multifarious activities was nothing but a bubble on that sea.

He was proud of belonging to the hidden groundmass of that race which carried on essential tasks, no matter under what form of government, no matter under what conditions of climate and soil: he had lived and multiplied; he had grown, created, not *acquired*, his and his children's daily bread: he had served God.

There are fewer nobler meditations on the dignity and greatness of the farmer's way of life than this. As in Hardy's *In Time of the Breaking of Nations* there is recognition of the mystical significance of the tilling of the soil, an awareness of labour which is part of a religious ceremony although the participant in the ceremony may have no physical feeling beyond that of fatigue and no emotion beyond hope of gain. And Grove, in articulating John Elliot's bitterness when he sees his family scatter from him, expresses admirably the emotion of the instinctive patriarch who at the end of his life finds himself abandoned by those whom he created expressly to carry on his work:

He had failed in the achievement of the second dream of his life. Half the purpose of his whole existence was gone. His children were scattered over two provinces of this country: they had freed themselves from the paternal rule: they were rebels in the house of their father: their aims were not what his had been. Their lives were evil; their lives were chaos; and through their lives, his own was chaos.

Here then, is a lofty theme, loftily uttered. But John Elliot never rises to the heights of tragic dignity which the theme demands. He is more often than not a petty, irritable old man who makes little attempt to understand his children, who resents their going from him without ever giving them much reason to wish to do otherwise. "Lear of the prairies" one of his more literate acquaintances calls him; and it is true that as Lear his creator visualized him. But the description is utterly inept. Lear is a Titan, the central figure in a struggle waged by the forces of good and evil in the awful forms of his own children. But the young Elliots inspire no awe; and scarcely any other emotion. They are negligible. So it is that old John Elliot crawls towards death, an abandoned and pathetic figure certainly, but about whom it is impossible to feel great anger or great grief. Too much of the time he and his family are little more than shadowy symbols, so far removed from the tremendous flesh and blood creations which surround Shakespeare's king as to make comparison a mockery.

Grove's failure in *Our Daily Bread* is chiefly a failure in comprehension. But his technique is also stumbling and uncertain. The narrative is episodic; and the steps in John Elliot's physical and spiritual breakdown are often indicated rather than described. Thus it is that we are sometimes confronted with a John Elliot years older and infinitely more embittered than the John Elliot of the preceding chapter. The force of V. S. Pritchett's dictum that it is less the business of the novelist to tell us what happened than to show us how it happened is illustrated, in a negative way, by Grove's failure to discuss fully the successive steps in John Elliot's decline and fall. We are compelled to take on faith what we would prefer to have fully described and explained to us; and our faith is not always strong enough.

The theme of *Our Daily Bread* is repeated with some variation in *Fruits of the Earth*. But Abe Spalding is a stronger character than John Elliot. Grove seems to have seen more clearly than in any of his earlier novels just what he wanted to make of his hero and to have gone about his task with considerable assurance. Like Elliot, Abe Spalding is an instinctive patriarch whose dream it is to own many acres of land and to be the father of many children who will care for the land after him. He homesteads in the marsh lands of Manitoba, is assisted at all times by that faculty of shrewd judgment without which even the hardest labour is likely to go unrewarded, and is soon recognized as the most important community citizen and a natural leader of men. But because Abe, like John Elliot, is a patriarch born out of due time, he and his family tend to grow apart. Between him and his wife and children there is little understanding, little sympathy. The great tragedy of Abe's life, in terms of a single incident, is the death of his young son Charlie, a dreamy sensitive youngster whom, rather illogically, Abe loves far more than he does any of his other three children. It is an irony probably quite unpremeditated on Grove's part that we are made to feel the inevitability of the favourite son, had he lived, being of all the children the least in sympathy with his father's ideals.

Spalding's re-emergence, in the last chapter or two of the book, as the community leader and strong man, is unconvincing. In spite of Grove's insistence that Spalding's morality is that of the majority of the settlers, that what he does is what "in a similar situation nine hundred and ninety-nine men out of a thousand would have done if they had dared," the reader is likely to have the uneasy feeling that he is witnessing the petty and temporary triumph of one who is not the local Hampden that his creator intended him to be.

The great weakness of *Fruits of the Earth,* considered not as a social document but as a work of art, is up to a point the weakness of *Our Daily Bread.* The people are names and little else besides. The daughters of Abe Spalding are not clearly distinguished from one another; and none of the score or more of minor characters who figure in the chronicle has sufficient personality to fix him for any length of time in the reader's mind. Nor indeed has Abe Spalding himself. But the fact that he is less a human being than a symbol is by design of his creator. For Abe Spalding is intended to be something more than an ordinary human being. It is no fault of Grove's design, but of his execution, that Spalding ends by being something less. In his autobiography, *In Search of Myself,* Grove gives us an account of the genesis of his hero. On his way to town across the open prairie with a load of grain, he saw one day far off on the crest of a hill, looking like a giant against the sunset, a man ploughing. The ploughman was the first human being Grove had seen in that part of the country. Grove spoke to him, and immediately regretted having done so. Too close association dispelled the magic of that first spectacular appearance against the flaming sunset:

Already, while he was standing by the side of the trail, with me reclining on top of my load of a hundred bushels of wheat; and more especially when he had uttered the last few words, he had not seemed to me to be quite the sort of giant I had imagined when he had first topped the crest of the hill. Yet, somehow, he had bodied forth for me the essence of the pioneering spirit which has settled the vast western plains and with which I had, through scores of concrete manifestations, become familiar during the preceding year.

The important thing was this. His first appearance, on top of the hill, had tripped a trigger in my imagination; he had become one with many others I had known; and an explosion had followed it in the nerve-centres of my brain because I had been ready for it. I had, for some time, been ready for the pains of birth. A, to me, momentous thing had happened; the figure of Abe Spalding, central to the book which, forty years later, was published under the title, *Fruits of the Earth,* had been born in my mind, fully armed as it were, and focalizing in itself a hundred features which I had noticed elsewhere. This man, this giant in body, if not mind and spirit, had furnished the physical features for a vision which had, so far, been incomplete because it had been abstract.

If I had seen the entirely casual occasion—that is all I can call him; he was not the prototype—of this figure again, if I had heard him speak as no doubt he had been used to speak, without relevance to my creation, that mental vision of mine would have been profoundly disturbed. A perfectly irrelevant actuality would have been superimposed upon my conception of a man who, as I saw him, had perhaps never lived; for he lacked that infusion of myself which makes him what he has become. From a type and a symbol, he would have become an individual; he would have been drained of the truth that lived in him; he would have become a mere fact.

This passage suggests Grove's power and his limitations. His view of man is philosophic; but in order to impose his view upon his readers he is impelled to see man not as an individual but as a symbol; and symbols, no matter how ingeniously created, are in the end lifeless things. Abe Spalding and John Elliot symbolize the patriarchal outlook. And that infusion of himself, which Grove says exists in Abe Spalding, is wholly inadequate to give reality to figures who in primary conception are intended to embody a view of life, rather than to *be* life itself.

This tendency to make his characters symbols rather than human beings is apparent in Grove's two novels which deal with settlement life in the northern Manitoba bush country. We are willing to accept Grove's statement that he actually knew a man so naive in sexual matters that up to the day of his marriage he had not known of the essential difference between male and female. But the fact that such a man may exist does not necessarily make him an acceptable hero of a novel. And Grove is not equal to the task which he sets himself in *Settlers of the Marsh*— that of making the central character, Niels Lindstedt, believable.

The hero of *The Yoke of Life*, Len Sterner, is for a time a recognizable human being, a frustrated farm boy seeking escape through education from a way of life which he finds repellent. But he too, becomes a symbol—of the ascetic spirit in a fleshly world—and the struggle between instinctive purity and sexual desire has little meaning because the protagonists, Len and Lydia, have almost nothing in common with recognizable human beings. Len's inhuman and hence unconvincing triumph through death is described in lofty and mystical terms; but the language of the philosopher is inadequate to make real the behaviour of beings remote from flesh and blood.

Because of his temperament Grove could never have been a great novelist. His autobiography, *In Search of Myself*, is the story of a man who, whatever his physical experiences, lived remote from the centre of life. He views his fellow men intellectually, never emotionally. He is a lonely, ascetic figure, repelled rather than attracted by humanity. A reading of *In Search of Myself*, serves to confirm one of the strongest impressions left by the novels, that Grove rarely, if ever, felt warmly towards any human being. Partly this impression may result from a horror on Grove's part of any kind of emotional display; but one is compelled to suspect, as in the case of his hero Len Sterner, an almost pathological shrinking from the animal that is man.

It is never enough that the novelist understand fully the technique of his art; or that he have the power to describe exciting incidents in vivid terms; or that he have a philosophical view of life which he expounds with eloquence; he must, above all else, know people intimately and be able to bring them to life in his pages. It is not possible to quarrel seriously with Virginia Woolf's assertion that all novels "deal with character, and that it is to express character, not to preach doctrines, sing songs, or celebrate the glories of the British Empire, that the form of the novel, so clumsy, verbose and undramatic, so rich, elastic and alive, has been evolved." But Grove's people are only occasionally human beings; the main figures are shadowy symbols around whom gather swarms of puppets —the Elliots and the Spaldings, and the neighbours who are seldom anything more than names, and occasionally grotesques like Mr. Pennycup and Mr. Suddaby and John

Elliot, Junior, who live a while in the memory because their remoteness from reality startles us into looking at them twice.

Grove's lack of sympathetic understanding of his fellow man is most obvious in his inability to reproduce with even a measurable degree of accuracy the ordinary conversation of ordinary people. Who can imagine any farm-boy—even one who loves literature—speaking, under stress of great emotion, as Len Sterner speaks to Lydia?

At last Len spoke. He did not look at her as he did so; he was intent only on finding the exact expression for the change which he had observed. His words seemed hardly to be addressed to her.

"Under the eaves of our sheep-shed," he said, "there hangs a pupa, attached to the boards by a fine, thin stalk. It is greyish brown and quite plain. It looks like the wood and has been there since last fall. Inside of it something is growing; and soon it will burst its shell. It will be a butterfly, checkered in gold and black. . . ."

His head moved and he looked full into her eyes. Little ripples of expectation ran along her spine. And then the bubble burst, precipitating her into a strange confusion of feelings.

"That is you," he said. "While you were at home you were the pupa. You have burst your shell and become a butterfly."

Or again, is it possible to conceive of any girl writing such a letter as Dr. Vanbruik shows to Abe Spalding, even after making all possible allowance for the extravagances of the jazz age?

My dear Vi,—Oh boy! I'm all tipsy and raring to go. Oh kid! Ma has relented. I'm going to attend a swell dance tomorrow night where the Tip Top Orchestra is playing. My togs are ready, compact filled, hair frizzed and all. Of course, Ma doesn't know; but Jack will be there with bells on. She thinks he's at Torquay yet. But this once I'm going to have a fling. Dash it, though! I was mad at Jack the other day, a week ago. You know that nifty compact he gave me last Xmas? He smashed it; and I gave him Hail Columbia. He'll bring me a new one tomorrow night; that'll be jake with me. Didn't I feel punk though!

Last night I met Agnes Strong on the ice. For the love of Pete! How that Jane carries on! I'd be ashamed of myself, honest to cats I would. You know Frank Smith the new sheik? He's sweet on me; and of course, I encourage him. Want some fun. But Agnes is cuckooed about him since he took her to a dance last week. It makes me puke to see her. Well, so long kiddo. Must ring off. Think of me tomorrow night, all dolled up. Frank says I'm a spiff looker. Hug me tight. See you in the funnies!—Pansy Blossom.

Here, unmistakably, one gets the impression of the author painstakingly gathering together a score of slang phrases, all of them popular in the early twenties, and weaving them together into a mosaic which, while containing not a word unsanctified by current usage, has in its totality nothing whatever in common with the way in which the youngsters of the jazz age expressed themselves. It is necessary only to compare the manner in which Ring Lardner handles the slang of the same period to comprehend the difference in artistic achievement between one whose knowledge of current jargon is academic and one who knows it through intimate acquaintance with those who create and speak it.

But although Grove is not a great novelist there are some things in his writing which are memorable. The tragedy of his artistic life is that so much of his work was done in a medium for which he had little talent. His best bits of writing are descriptive and philosophical rather than narrative. In a milieu less harassing it is possible that he might have been a distinguished essayist. He has a keen eye and the power to record accurately what he sees. There are, too, some fine passages of philosophic meditation in the novels, such as the reflection, in *Our*

Daily Bread, on the farmer's way of life; and in the same book, the sombre moving soliloquy on death expressed in the form of the thoughts which pass through John Elliot's mind as he sits by the bedside of his dying son-in-law, which do much to make the banal dialogue and inadequately realized characterization tolerable. But it is not possible to read Grove's two collections of descriptive pieces, *Over Prairie Trails* and *The Turn of the Year,* without feeling that his best work lies in just such things as these. In them he is able to combine an accurate eye for description and the philosophic strain so strong in him without impeding the development of plot or characterization. The pity of it is that Grove, either because of economic pressure or a mistaken estimate of his own powers, felt impelled to work in a medium which was not suited to his peculiar talents.

Not that we would willingly give up any of the novels of the Canadian West which Grove wrote. Imperfect though they are they reflect a maturity of intellect lacking in most of our fiction. Grove is not a great novelist, for the power to create living people was denied him; but he brought a cultured and philosophic mind to the contemplation of the Western scene, and an eye for specific detail which will make his work a valuable source of information to the rural historian of the future. His statement of purpose in writing *Fruits of the Earth*—"to infuse a dramatic interest into agricultural operations and that attendant rural life thereof"—holds true of all his Western novels. He failed to infuse adequately the dramatic interest, but his record of "agricultural operations and the attendant rural life thereof" is one of the most accurate in Canadian fiction.

A FIERCE PURITAN

A. L. PHELPS

A Canadian writer whom the few have acclaimed and the many ignored, Frederick Philip Grove was once described to me as the best unread author in Canada. I think Grove, who died in 1948, would have taken a wry satisfaction from both puttings of the case. In one of his bitter moments he said that perhaps he was writing for posterity; certainly he was not writing for his own time. He left behind him two volumes of descriptive essays, one volume of sharply reflective critical essays called, characteristically, *It Needs To Be Said*, two volumes of autobiography—one oblique under a fictional veil, one direct, personal and poignant—and nearly a dozen novels, in published form or in manuscript. Two books have been written on him. His work has been the subject of many critical essays. Most Canadians reasonably knowledgable about books would say he is our most important literary figure. Yet, so saying, they might never have read him; and so Grove remains for most Canadians acknowledged, but unread—an author with a reputation and no public.

This is a rather strange situation in regard to a presumably competent author. I think if I open it out and discuss it a bit some interesting things about Canada and the literary conditions in Canada may be made plain.

I first met Philip Grove in the early twenties. That seems a long time ago. I met him because I sought him out—I sought him out because I had read his first book, a volume of essays called *Over Prairie Trails*. And I read that book because a learned old Scotsman, who had been a missionary among the Blackfoot Indians and had since retired to be a librarian in the college in Winnipeg where I was teaching, said to me one day "Here's a book. Read

From "Frederick Philip Grove" in *Canadian Writers* by A. L. Phelps (Toronto: McClelland and Stewart, 1951), 36-42. By permission of McClelland and Stewart.

it. It's something unusual in Canada—a piece of writing with power and beauty in it." Dr. MacLean—the grand old boy, camper by prairie trails, student of Indian philology, author—who, though tamed a bit as a college librarian, still chewed tobacco and spat the juice behind the denominational college radiators, was right. Grove's work had quality.

That spring there was a Provincial Teachers' Convention in Winnipeg. Grove, who was then a school teacher in one of the small prairie towns, attended. I saw him first across a room in the Convention Hotel. He was taller than those about him. He stooped a little as he listened to a conversation. He looked Scandinavian. His face was both rough-hewn and fine. I could see his gestures and catch the rise and fall of his resonant talk with a foreign accent. One felt that a man was standing there among the teachers. . . . I think much of Grove's writing will have an eventual public. Grove himself, as writer, will stand inevitably in the Canadian literary tradition. No writer in Canada has worked so assiduously, so continuously, so passionately against such odds at the job of writing. True, he never broke beyond the limitations imposed by the fact that he was writing in English and not in his native tongue. He never got away from the tradition of the over-long nineteenth century novel. I have in my possession handwritten and typed manuscripts which run to hundreds of thousands of words. The fierce puritan in Grove seemed to drive him to write on and on and on in the attempt to fulfil in expression every possible expansion of his material. Publishers' readers would say "He is good. There is grand stuff in him, but he is writing out of touch with the mode of his time." All this is true, but, whether he is read just now or not, Grove's passionate absorption in the craft of letters has enriched the tone of literary culture in Canada. And some day, perhaps some day soon, editorial insight will abstract from the mass of his work the selections which will present in agreeable compass that strength and beauty in his work which old Dr. MacLean, the Blackfoot missionary, was so sure about.

I am inclined to think that the failure of Grove to gain a public contemporary with himself was in part the failure of Canadian criticism. We are a dispersed population in Canada and we lack the kind of book reviewing in local journals here and there across the country which creates that climate of expectation and critical appraisal in which a somewhat difficult and unusual author lives. Furthermore, in Grove's day we had not developed the techniques of publishers' ballyhoo and aggressive salesmanship which might, irrespective of merit, have launched one or other of Grove's books among the drawing room and cocktail coteries.

As a readable book, indeed as a fascinating story of hobo wanderings across the face of the United States, I can recommend *A Search for America*. It is full of incident, fabulous, fantastic and homely. And there is a man in that book. There is also an America in it.

Among the novels, I suggest *Our Daily Bread*. It is a slow-moving, rather heavily written book. But it has accumulation and power in it, and there are one or two pieces of descriptive and reflective writing that are events for the reader. It is a story of Saskatchewan and of the break-up of a farm family under the impact of urban influences. An agricultural tradition decays and, for Grove, there is an accompaniment of character disintegration. Much of the book is the record of what Grove saw taking place in the changing culture of the Canadian West.

One other novel I should like to mention. It is Grove's first published novel, called *Settlers of the Marsh*. I mention this book because of what Grove himself says of it. The comment is a clue to much in Grove. He says:

Personally, I thought it a great book; personally, I loved it as a beautiful thing; but—to this day I am not sure that it conveys to others what it conveys to me. If it does, nobody has ever said so.

I can also recommend Grove's book of descriptive essays *Over Prairie Trails*. The book is mainly the detailed, meticulously observed record of winter drives, sometimes behind plunging teams in smothering blizzards and sometimes with ease and speed in moonlit crystal clear zero weather. I think Grove has, as we say, "done" snow in *Over Prairie Trails* as it has not been done before in literature.

One last word. If you want the moving, too self-preoccupied story of this partially self-thwarted artist read *In Search of Myself* by Frederick Philip Grove.

A PEAK GLINTING IN THE SUN

WILFRID EGGLESTON

. . . Grove in his lifetime tried many literary forms: the novel, the short story, the essay, the lyric, autobiography, literary criticism, allegory—even the detective story and the juvenile. One of the pleasant surprises to any student of Grove is his excellence in some of the minor fields. Popular attention has been focused generally on Grove's longer fiction. His most perfect work, however, is almost certainly to be found in his nature essays, his short stories, his literary criticism and his lyrics. His most perennially interesting work is to be found in his two books of autobiography. However, it is as a Canadian novelist that Grove is generally presented today, and for the remainder of this talk I shall confine myself mainly to that part of his work.

Grove passionately wanted to write a great novel or group of great novels; I think there is no doubt about that. He greatly admired the masters in this field: Turgenev,

Excerpts from "Frederick Philip Grove" in *Our Living Tradition: Seven Canadians* (edited by Claude T. Bissell; Toronto: University of Toronto Press, 1957), 105-127. Originally a lecture at Carleton University. By permission of Wilfrid Eggleston.

Conrad, Meredith, Hardy, Tolstoi. He envied Hamsun, Rolvaag, Thomas Mann and Galsworthy their contemporary successes. He realized that of all the literary art forms, the novel was the one currently in fashion, and the one which might win him a place among the immortals.

Possibly he guaranteed his own failure in advance by setting his sights impossibly high. "What is the measure of a writer's greatness?" William Faulkner was asked recently. "The splendour of failure," he replied. If Grove really wanted to be the Joseph Conrad or Thomas Hardy of Canada—and there is some evidence that he so aspired—it can be contended that defeat was ensured in advance.

He possessed, certainly, some of the qualities of a great literary artist. He had a thorough intellectual grasp of the nature of tragedy, as can be seen from his essays in *It Needs to be Said*. He possessed an unusually intimate acquaintance with the outstanding literary works of Europe. He was an acute student of nature. He was versed in anthropology and archaeology. His writing style was adequate. He confessed that when he was writing *Over Prairie Trails* he realized that he had at bottom no language peculiarly his own. Instead, he had half a dozen of them. But this, he was shrewd enough to see, was a disadvantage and even a misfortune. "I lacked," he said, "that *limitation* which is best for the profound penetration of the soul of a language." But such a limitation was not in my opinion the critical one in his ambition to write great novels. For that he needed one gift above all, the divine gift of being able to give his creations abundant life. Had he possessed that gift in high degree, any stiffness in his style would have been readily forgotten.

As it is, the occasional clumsiness of his expression is not a serious defect. He mastered the essentials of English grammar, and his essay style rose at times to grandeur. His vocabulary could be painfully precise, and did not often become elegant or notably felicitous. For a novelist perhaps his most serious lack was mastery of the vernacular.

He had a very limited ear for the colloquial rhythms of common speech. Indeed, it may be that his hardness of hearing and the effect it had in making him something of a recluse robbed him of the opportunities of registering often and deeply the raw stuff out of which a fine novelist creates his conversations. Grove's dialogue, especially the speech attributed to the younger generation, is one of the weaker elements of his fictional technique. Above all, he lacked humour.

He was handicapped, too, I think, in failing to find in time friendly critics and editors who might have helped him greatly to attain virtuosity in literary style. He was essentially self-taught. When he did find a sympathetic editor in Lorne Pierce, he was fifty-three and it was too late. By then Grove, with a stubbornness which you may think showed his artistic integrity, refused to change a line or even a word of his script, unless his editor or publisher was adamant, and not always then. He would withdraw the manuscript rather than yield. On balance perhaps this was wise, and it certainly protected Grove against those publishers who might have urged him to compromise and popularize his work in the interests of sales. But any conscientious editor, reading Grove's published work, itches at times to make minor textual changes here and there, to remove irritating flaws in diction or sentence construction. To be completely fair, some of these were due to excessive haste in preparing manuscripts for the printers.

A more serious handicap for the novelist has been suggested by both Edward McCourt and Isabel Skelton. Was Grove passionately interested in the fate and welfare of mankind? He said himself that he loved nature more than man. Did he really love people well enough to understand them? His portrayal of certain types of humanity was superb, particularly old men, masterful and ruthless, and men in their senile decay. But when he tried to portray adolescents or young lovers he usually faltered. Mrs.

Skelton, in an article in the *Dalhousie Review*, drew attention to a passage in one of Grove's literary essays: "I abominate," he wrote—and this is strong language from him—"the common love-story—the story of pre-nuptial love—almost as violently as I abhor the gramophone, the telephone or the radio. In life, both young men and young maids are peculiarly uninteresting at a time when they see each other as they are not."

Again, I think it was most unlucky that Grove did not receive some encouragement in his fiction while he was still a young man. It was not until he was fifty-four that his first novel was published. Most of the world's great novelists have been about ready to sign off at that age. He himself says that the last but one burst of miraculous creativeness had occurred a few months before. Who knows what work he might have done in the novel if he had won success twenty years earlier, before his deafness had advanced, and while he still mingled with young people and caught the nuances and rhythms of their talk?

The idea that there is any connection between the age of a novelist and his prospects of worthy literary offspring may be challenged. I believe that if I had the time I could make out a strong case. At any rate it is demonstrable that at least 90 per cent of the novels the world regards as great were not only written but published by the time the writer reached the age of fifty-four, when Grove published his *first* novel. Moreover, I toss in for what it is worth an assertion of William Allen White, the famous editor of the *Emporia Gazette*, that "fiction is a matter of glands." When one is no longer interested in sex, Mr. White contended, and when anger has been succeeded by mellowness, then it is time to quit writing fiction.

How different it might have been for Frederick Philip Grove, if when he submitted to publishers an early draft of *A Search for America* in the middle nineties, he had found a sympathetic editor of the calibre of Lorne Pierce or Hugh Eayrs. He might have become a published novelist thirty years before he did, and his whole career might have been profoundly affected for the better.

It is idle to speculate thus. What does matter is that despite all handicaps, despite ill health, his desolation at the untimely death of his daughter, the indifference of the reading public and other discouragements, he persevered. Using time that was largely won for him by the heroic assistance of his wife, he succeeded in writing and publishing no less than seven novels before his death. I propose now to look briefly at each of these in turn.

Settlers of the Marsh—Grove's first novel, published in 1925 and with two editions—is set in the bushland north of the open wheat plains of Manitoba. Grove called it a "garbled extract" of what was intended to be a three-volume work called *Pioneers*. He thought highly of it: "Personally," he wrote, "I thought it a great book; personally, I loved it as a beautiful thing." But, he added, its publication became a public scandal. As I have reported, it was denounced as obscene. The book never had a chance as a trade proposition; what sale it had was surreptitious. In another place, Grove said that the publication of *Settlers of the Marsh* proved an unmitigated disaster. It is not true, however, as has been reported, that its publication made it impossible for him any longer to find a position as teacher in Manitoba. His increasing hardness of hearing had already terminated his teaching career. Desmond Pacey thinks that though this was in some ways Grove's most ambitious novel it was not, in an artistic sense, his most successful. George Herbert Clarke and Carleton Stanley thought highly of it. W. E. Collin rather surprisingly finds in the novel not so much a story of pioneers in rural Manitoba as a symbolic ritual tale harking back to pagan days. Niels Lindstedt, the central figure, is a peasant type of grail questor, says Collin, and Grove's mystery is really a medieval romance. Isabel Skelton has mixed feelings about it. I come from a recent re-reading of all of Grove's novels with the conviction that this is his most artistic achievement, deeply felt and on the whole most successfully realized.

A Search for America, first published in 1927, is a blend of autobiography and fiction; it is doubtful if we shall ever know how much is history and how much is romance. The most popular of all Grove's published works, it has run through several editions and is still selling in a school abridgement. It was the earliest in composition of all of his books, and the style is easier and more flexible, perhaps as a result. Perhaps it caught a bit more of his youthful liveliness and fertility of imagination. When it appeared, Fred Jacob, the Toronto critic, wrote: "Of all the Canadian books that I have read, it is the only one I should like to have written." Isabel Skelton seems to have liked this novel best of all. It has a dramatic lifelike variety, she wrote, which does not pall. "It is a unique Pilgrim's Progress, partly autobiographical, partly allegoric, showing how the author's outlook upon life became changed by the encounters he had with all sorts and conditions of men in the United States and Canada." Carleton Stanley says he has a higher opinion of the book than the author of it had. Grove, indeed, thought it was artistically his weakest book. It is a masculine book. There is no love interest at all, and the few feminine figures in it are casual and shadowy.

Our Daily Bread was brought out by Macmillan in 1928 and sold very well for a Canadian novel: over 3,000 copies in the first year. The setting is in what Grove calls the land of the sunset; bare, naked prairie hills, sun-baked, rain-washed . . . the Saskatchewan terrain, say, between Moose Jaw and Swift Current. Grove would have preferred to call it *Lear of the Prairie*, had Turgenev not anticipated him. This gives some idea of the theme. It is the story of a pathetic old man and his indifferent, ungrateful children who go their own selfish ways. Pacey thought highly of it; writing in 1945 he said: "Better novels than this may some day be written in Canada, but I do not believe they have been written yet." George Herbert Clarke is critical of its organization, but thinks that the final chapters redeem the book, especially the concluding account of the "grimly masterful hero's old age and death." This is a view I can personally endorse. Isabel Skelton thinks that Grove found a congenial theme in the old man's decay, but she feels that the reader, like his children, has lost interest in him before the end. He lacks Lear's majesty, his endowment of heart and spirit is so meagre that his fate appears less than tragic, she contends. He is not a noble figure defeated by circumstance, but a selfish man betrayed by his own selfishness. Edward McCourt comes to a similar conclusion.

In *The Yoke of Life*, published by Macmillan in 1930, we are again in the bush country of *Settlers of the Marsh*. This novel met with a cool reception, both from critics and from the book buyers. Only 571 copies were sold in the first year of publication and virtually none thereafter. Lorne Pierce called it a Canadian *Jude the Obscure*—and a pale copy at that. McCourt thinks that the hero, having begun as a recognizable human being, ends up as a symbol. Mrs. Skelton feels that the novel begins with the best opening chapter in all of Grove's writings, but that the theme, which is pre-nuptial love, is so abhorrent to the author that all comes to grief. The foundation for the existence of the lovers, she says, has been evolved out of theories, and in no scene does the novel hold the reader as a page of life and truth. Desmond Pacey is kinder, though he too thinks of it as a failure, even if a magnificent failure. Carleton Stanley called it a great book when it appeared, and in spite of a chorus of disapproval, he stood by his guns. "I not only think so still," he said fifteen years after its publication, "I am more struck with its greatness, its eminence in tragic pathos, every time I re-read it."

For *Fruits of the Earth*, published in 1933 by J. M. Dent in England and Canada, I have been unable to obtain an accurate note on sales. Grove himself says that it, like *The Yoke of Life*, was a commercial failure, that it fell flat. I do not myself care very much for it, but others value it as an accurate picture of settlement and farm life in the flat lands of southern Manitoba. McCourt praises in it the accuracy and maturity of Grove's approach to agricultural life on the prairies. Pacey thinks that if the ending were stronger, this would be Grove's finest book and that even so, it is surpassed only by *Our Daily Bread*. Mrs. Skelton regrets that the author found no beauty, no grace, no laughter or tears in the farm life of Manitoba. She thinks this is written in the most pedestrian and unimaginative style of all his novels. Nor, she says, does this academic man understand the simple unsophisticated rural Manitoba community. However, Pacey finds more sheer speed in its movement than in any other of the novels, and George Herbert Clarke points out that it is the closest of all to the physical details and social problems of the prairie. Perhaps it is because I spent my own boyhood and early youth on a prairie farm that I am less generous in my praise of this particular book. The surface activity of such a farm is well described: I miss its soul and essence and the inward life of the pioneer settler.

Two Generations is a farm novel with an Ontario setting. It was written after Grove had purchased his dairy farm at Simcoe, and by then he was already in his sixties. He was unable to find a publisher, and at last printed it himself, after selling sufficient copies by subscription to cover most of the outlay. It is a less ambitious work than most, quieter and more mellow. Grove himself called it "a mere trifle," but it bears the marks of much devoted craftsmanship and careful editing. Critics have labelled it one of his "pleasant" books. Pacey does not think it possesses the importance of the prairie novels, but Dr. W. J. Alexander rated it as "incomparably the best thing" Grove had done. I find it easy and pleasant to read, but it does not move me much, and some of the episodes and more than a bit of the dialogue are quite unconvincing. The theme is a favourite with Grove, and appears to stem from his own relations with his father; it is, once more, the clash between a domineering father and his wilful off-spring.

The Master of the Mill, the last of Grove's novels to be published to date, appeared in 1944. Macmillan's figures show very modest but persistent sales: 650 in the year of publication, 400 the following year, smaller numbers in subsequent years—33, for example, as late as 1955/6, ten years after publication. This is Grove's only experiment in depicting the industrial scene. The setting is a gigantic flour-milling industry at the head of the Great Lakes. Grove did all the research for it as early as 1928. In 1934 he accepted advance royalties against it from J. M. Dent and Sons, completing the manuscript in hope of spring publication in 1935. Dent's English reader called it "a book on the grand scale, a book that demands admiration for its scope and its courage in tackling big and contem-porary themes," but he did not recommend publication, and the manuscript was returned to Grove. It rested on his shelves for nearly a decade and appeared first in a limited edition in 1944. It is one of the few Grove books still obtainable. Lorne Pierce did not care for it. He wrote, "Only in *The Master of the Mill* can he be said to have produced a failure. It is melodramatic and unreal. His determination to tell all results in his telling little." Pacey calls it a "powerful" novel, but does not consider it Grove's masterpiece. Dr. Clarke says that the value of this novel depends upon its ideas and upon a few dramatic episodes, but adds that the constant effort to fuse fiction with thesis and exposition and the frequent troublesome shiftings in point of view impair its validity and power as a work of art. Personally, I found it an interesting and powerful experiment which impresses even in its failure.

What is Grove's place in Canadian literature? This is a difficult question which I should prefer to leave unattempted, but perhaps cannot evade.

He was never a popular author, and his name is not widely familiar today. Only three of his seven novels sold enough copies to cover publishers' costs, only two are currently in print. Any one of Ralph Connor's early novels sold more copies than the total sales of all those of Grove. *Anne of Green Gables* sold more copies in 1909 than the cumulative sales of all Grove's novels in thirty years. It follows that Grove's novels as a whole were not profitable to him in a financial sense. He made a net profit from *Our Daily Bread*, and with better luck *A Search for America* might have continued to bring in some income for years. But at best, in his own estimation, his lifetime of creative writing did not bring him in as much as two cents an hour, though he applied himself to it with rare devotion and industry for nearly fifty years.

Grove hungered after popular approval, but he would not compromise his art to seek for it. When in later years even his small public of the twenties seemed to peter out, he stoutly declared that he would appeal to posterity: only the future could decide whether his work was to count for anything in this world. It made him laugh, he said, when a book-reviewer called a novel of his a classic. "Why doesn't he wait a few hundred years," he commented, "before using such a grandiloquent word?" Grove thought that the artist should always build his work as if it were meant to last through the centuries.

We cannot, of course, foresee what future generations of Canadians will think of Grove. We can, however, get some idea of his stature from the testimony of his contemporaries. I have quoted favourable comments from such diverse sources as Fred Jacob, Isabel Skelton, Desmond Pacey, W. E. Collin, Carleton Stanley, W. J. Alexander, E. A. McCourt, George Herbert Clarke and Lorne Pierce. Watson Kirkconnell, Barker Fairley and A. L. Phelps were his friends and admirers. A small man would not have attracted the attention of such a cluster of literary critics. He was awarded the Lorne Pierce Medal of the Royal Society of Canada in 1934. His autobiography won the Governor-General's medal. Two universities recognized his achievement by the award of honorary degrees.

Indirect tribute of a high order was paid to him in 1948. A committee of eight judges, representing five cultural societies, was asked by UNESCO to compile a list of Canada's 100 best books. Each judge submitted an independent list of 100; when these were collated, the resulting list contained 350. Frederick Philip Grove was represented in the 350 by 9 books—six novels, two books of essays and his autobiography. No other Canadian author scored so high. This list of 350 was reduced to the requested 100. The smaller list included two of Grove's novels and one book of essays: more than any other Canadian writer except Charles G. D. Roberts who matched Grove for first place.

. . . "What then is tragic?" Frederick Philip Grove asked in one of his essays. "To have greatly tried and to have failed; to have greatly wished and to be denied." But like Prometheus, even in our failure we exult, because we have fought with courage against the odds of life. In his later years, it is true, Grove sometimes yielded to despair and even declared his life to be an abject failure. Indeed, he set out to write his autobiography with the avowed reason of explaining to somebody—to whom?—why, after such bright early promise he had accomplished so little. Somewhere, he quotes Schiller:

Into the ocean, with a thousand masts the stripling sails,
Subdued, on a salvaged skiff, into the haven drifts the grey-
    beard.

But is such a deflating experience peculiar to Grove? I do not think that the pessimism of his last years was warranted.

Prophecy, wrote the late J. W. Dafoe, is the most gratuitous form of error. Even so, I would dare to predict that Grove's reputation will grow. Future generations of Canadians will wonder about the literary pioneers. Grove was the first serious exponent of realism in our fiction. He left behind him a few exquisite essays, a few penetrating pages of criticism, some powerful short stories, two fascinating books of autobiography and a group of moving lyrics. There was, perhaps, no flawless masterpiece among his seven novels, but in some of the fragmentary and truncated efforts there is more sheer power and vitality than in any of the polished minor successes of Canadian fiction. Time has a fashion of eroding the weaker materials away, and leaving the peaks glinting in the sun.

A NOVELIST AS POET

THOMAS SAUNDERS

On July 17, 1962, the University of Manitoba made arrangements to purchase from Mrs. Catherine Grove, widow of the late Frederick Philip Grove, a number of manuscripts of her husband's work. These included both published and unpublished material—novels, short stories, articles, addresses, notebooks, essays, sketches, letters, and poems. The collection also includes some reviews and comment on Grove's work.

Of the published novels six are represented: *Our Daily Bread, Fruits of the Earth, Two Generations, Consider Her Ways, The Master of the Mill* and *Settlers of the Marsh.* There is, in addition, the children's story, *The Adventures of Leonard Broadus,* which serialized in the United Church paper, *The Canadian Boy,* in 1940; and a number of short stories and articles.

"A Novelist as Poet: Frederick Philip Grove" by Thomas Saunders, in *Dalhousie Review,* XLIII (Summer 1963), 235-241. By permission of Thomas Saunders and *Dalhousie Review.*

Unpublished works include *The Weatherhead Fortunes*
("History of a Small Town"), *The Poet's Dream* (or *The
Canyon*), *Murder in the Quarry,* a manuscript of short
stories entitled *Tales from the Margin* and a collection of
poems. To these must be added a number of other short
stories, articles, essays and sketches.

Though by no means a complete record of material by
and about Grove, the whole adds up to what must be considered the beginning of a definitive collection. It is to the
University of Manitoba library that Grove scholars and
researchers must now turn for much of the material on
which their work will be based.

There is, of course, an appropriateness in the University
of Manitoba having acquired these documents. It was in
Manitoba that Grove "found" himself as a writer. Here
much of his best work was done, and here he first found
publication in the early twenties. His discoverers, indeed,
were men of the university (or of one of its affiliates,
United College)—Arthur L. Phelps, Watson Kirkconnell,
and the late Dr. J. H. Riddell. Grove took his B.A. degree
at the university, which subsequently honoured him with
an honorary degree as well. When death claimed him it
was to Manitoba that his body was returned—to rest beside
his daughter in the little cemetery at Rapid City where
both he and his wife had taught school.

What the documents acquired by the university will
mean in terms of future research only time, of course, will
tell. Grove was a controversial character during his lifetime; he has remained a controversial figure since his
death. The controversy has raged not only about his life
but about his work. He has been described by one set of
critics as a great writer, by others as a poor one. By some,
both as a person and author, he has been considered something of a fake. But both he and his work continue to
command interest; and, among not a few knowledgeable
people, they continue to command respect.

It is not the intention here to become involved in this

controversy or to make an assessment of the value of the manuscripts and typescripts now in University of Manitoba's possession. To make such an assessment (entirely aside from the question of Grove's merit as a writer) would require a more detailed analysis of the documents than the writer has so far been able to give them. One of the manuscript collections, however, is worthy of immediate comment, and I therefore deal at present with the poems.

Not many people are aware of Grove as a poet, and the manuscript now housed in the University of Manitoba collection would not encourage rhapsodies over his achievements in verse. Yet it is interesting to note his apparently life-long respect for poetry and his attempts to write it. For, while most of what is contained in the University of Manitoba collection was written after 1927, and was apparently motivated by the death of his daughter, there are indications that he dabbled in poetry during most of his writing life. A date on one of the poems, indeed, suggests that it was written in Nova Scotia as early as 1909.

Grove's interest in writing poetry, however, does not seem to have given him any great mastery of the craft. (Perhaps it would be more accurate to say that he reveals mastery of the craft but little beyond that—technical proficiency within imitative limits but not the true poet's ability to give words implications and ramifications beyond themselves.) In 1922, after reading *Over Prairie Trails,* Arthur Phelps wrote him: "You give us the observation of the scientist made with the eye of the poet." Phelps was enthusiastic over the poetic quality of Grove's prose. But when Grove set out consciously to write poetry, he was not so successful and Phelps was less enthusiastic. "I don't like your verse so well," he wrote in the same letter—a judgment which, after reading the typescripts in the University of Manitoba collection, I am prepared to support.

Written almost exclusively in unvarying iambic pentameters, Grove's verse, over all, while technically correct, is pedestrian and dull. It seldom gets off the ground. It is obviously imitative and much of it could as well have been written in prose. For example:

> I never thought a day could be so stale
> And drag its weary hours as this one did.

Whatever else these lines may be, they are not poetry. At times he is positively banal. It is hard to imagine, for example, anything pretending to be poetry that could be much worse than this:

> Come, let us sit behind this wind-built dune
> And look upon the slumbering lagoon.

But not everything he offers as poetry is on this low plane and, aside from their merit as verse, the poems are not without value in assessing the man. They give us something of his basic philosophy, throw light on the content and form of the novels; and in the long poem, "The Dirge," written after the death of his daughter, we have as searching an account as we are likely to have of his emotion and thought during what was undoubtedly one of the most tragic and critical periods in his life. This poem, though philosophically more pessimistic than anything that could have come from Tennyson, is reminiscent in its form—though not in its rhyme-scheme—of "In Memoriam." This may make its sincerity suspect by some readers. Long poems in the form of dirges over someone we profess to love can have an aspect of falseness about them. But from those who knew Grove at the time of his daughter's death, and from all we know of the rapport that seems to have existed between father and daughter, plus the natural affection that can be assumed, this does not seem to have been the case here. Grove, like many artists, seems to have been an essentially selfish man. His tendency was to *use* people, even those closest to him. But there is no evidence of this in his relationship with his daughter. She seems to have occupied a special place in his affections, and he gave himself to her as to perhaps no other person.

Before considering the long poem occasioned by her death, however, it may be well to examine some of his other verse. The first poem in the typescripts, entitled "Preface," states his purpose in writing the poems that welled up in him following this tragedy:

> To tell posterity in accents terse
> How one man felt whom God had bent and rent.

But there is nothing terse in what follows. In his verse, as in his prose, Grove took his time and was unwilling to be hurried. His nearest approach to terseness is in his description of the world, his outlook on which is dark indeed:

> This world?
> A synonym for prison bars.

But although he feels that life is basically harsh and unjust, he refuses to bow to it or to take comfort in the thought of a kindly providence in which he cannot believe. His concept of life, for himself as for the main characters in his novels, is essentially tragic and is nowhere better expressed than in the poem, "The Rebel's Confession of Faith":

> I still decline
> Thus to be mothered by a providence
> Whose kindness is less provident than mine,
> Whose justice is but bartering recompense.
>
> I'd rather have my weakness than its strength;
> I'd rather stand, a beggar, on my own
> Than in reward receive the breadth and length
> Of worlds or kingdoms. . . .

It is in passages such as this, where feeling and conviction are both strong, that he comes closest to being a poet. Sometimes, in the midst of otherwise pedestrian writing, he holds us with a single line, as in his description of "The sleeping phantoms of a fossil past."

But it is the long poem dedicated to his daughter (about two-thirds of which was published in *The Canadian Forum* in its issue of April, 1932) that is most self-revealing and contains most of his better lines. The girl, Phyllis May, died at Rapid City when she was barely twelve years of age. The loss of the child seems to have touched Grove as perhaps no other event in his life. All the other hardships he had been confronted with were as nothing compared with this. His heroic attitude toward life, never broken by adversity, came nearest to the breaking-point at this time; and the verse which resulted, if not without its flaws, is in many respects worthy of its subject. It has, I believe, a quality of deep sincerity; and for Grove, in writing it, it must have acted as a sort of catharsis, giving relief to his burdened mind.

In it we find the first expression of his desire to be buried beside his daughter when his time comes:

> Sleep without fear, my child, not long alone:
> For there is room for me, too, in that throng.
> Some quarry even now grows my own stone.
> Here will I come, nor will I tarry long.

Grove had been a wanderer throughout much of his life. After the death of his daughter he could be a wanderer no more. As he expresses it,

> No country, so far, claimed me all her own;
> My emblem was the sail. . . .

But his child's death changed all that:

> Now am I anchored; and forever now
> Must here I tarry. For a woman gave
> A child to me; and to the ground I bow;
> My roots are growing down into a grave.

There seems little doubt that, for Grove, the death of his daughter was the black night of the soul. It was a darkness out of which he found it hard to climb. Even St. Paul's trinity of faith, hope, and love held little comfort for him. Of faith and hope his entire philosophy of life had tended to rob him; and, in his bereavement, he felt that even love had failed. His love for his daughter had no power to break the bonds of death. His statement of this gives us the darkest lines in a dark poem:

> But Love, the greatest, proving destitute
> Of power to lift the lid from off the tomb,
> The bauble Hope lay broken; Faith was mute
> And mocked itself by shrugging, Faith in whom?

But something in him clings to the thought that death cannot have the last word. Beauty changes but never dies. Shelley's thought about the young Keats comes to him, and it is Shelley's lines that are engraved on the tombstone of his daughter's grave:

> She is a portion of the loveliness
> Which once she made more lovely.

His own, more verbose, expression of this runs:

> What wafts the wind upon its midnight breath?
> It bears, transformed, soft rain from out the sea
> And spins a message that there is no death,
> That what once was, transformed, shall ever be.

In all his poems, this is as positive a statement on the great issues of life and death as Grove ever allowed himself. There is no suggestion of a belief in personal immortality—only an assertion of the unextinguishable nature of beauty. It is still the tragic concept that prevails—a belief in the earthly immortality of the values he cherishes, values that may be buffeted by an improvident providence but can never be totally destroyed.

This, of course, is the basic philosophy that supported Grove all through his life and through the tribulations of his writing career. The long years of writing, in what was virtually a cultural vacuum, with little or no hope of publication, may be partly explained through the fact that he was a compulsive writer. But there is also this—

his unfailing belief in the rightness of what he was doing, his faith in the permanence of its value, his conviction of the survival of the best that was in him and the world despite tragedy. These things go a long way to explain both the fact and the nature of his writing; and in revealing them, the poems illuminate both his life and his prose.

It may be true that the poems, as poems, leave something to be desired. It may be equally true that their publication in book form would add little to Grove's literary reputation—they might even detract from it. But they should still be of inestimable value not only to the research scholar but to the ordinary reader who is interested in Grove the man, as well as in Grove the writer. Besides throwing light on his thought and character, and being a mirror of his emotion and mind in the aftermath of perhaps the most tragic episode in his life, in condensed form they illustrate the philosophy that informed the corpus of his published work and motivated the delineation of his principal characters. Here, in essence, are Abe Spalding, Niels Lindstedt, John Elliot and all the others.

But more than this, the poems are a clue to the nineteenth-century influences that shaped Grove's writing career. Because his first book, *Over Prairie Trails,* was not published until 1922, and his first novel, *Settlers of the Marsh,* until 1925, it is sometimes assumed that Grove belongs to a much later era than he does. Adverse judgments on his writing have sometimes been made on this false premise. It is conveniently forgotten that Grove started his first draft of *Latter Day Pioneers,* the trilogy out of which *Settlers of the Marsh* was literally hacked, as early as 1892.[1] He had been cut adrift from the European culture in which he had been nurtured some time before that, and there were few literary influences available to play on his life during the long years in which he worked

---

[1] If writing this article today the author would rewrite this sentence as follows: "It is conveniently forgotten that Grove came to this continent in the 1890s and that he wrote for thirty years before he found publication."

as a farmhand, following the harvests from Kansas to the Canadian prairies, until he settled down as a schoolteacher in a series of Manitoba towns.

The poems reflect this. They are imitative, not of twentieth-century, but of nineteenth-century models. As such, they reflect the same influences that shaped his prose. But they are not imitative of the easy optimism that marked much nineteenth-century writing. They are marked by the tragic manner and a philosophy and concept of realism—the same philosophy and concept that informs his prose. This, even in the 1920s, was something new in Canadian writing. Indeed, it is a measure of Grove's greatness—and a reflection on the development of the art of the novel in Canada up to that time—that, when *Settlers of the Marsh* was finally published, it still broke new ground by introducing the novel of realism into the literature of this country. (Grove may have arrived late as a published writer, but—to use his own phrase—he was still a "latter day pioneer.")

The poems have special value in reminding us of these things. Taken by themselves, and judged only as poetry, they may be regarded as having minimal significance. But seen in relation to Grove the writer, and Grove the man, they help illumine both his life and his published work.

EXCERPTS FROM SELECTED REVIEWS

Over Prairie Trails (1922)

... These observations, written with real distinction of style, have been put into a book which strikes me as being a unique production. Mr. Grove has jotted down details which would be voted by the average reader as trifling and tiresome, but the author of this book was not writing to please Tom, Dick, and Harry; he was writing to please himself, and all those who belong to the tribe of William Wordsworth. For there can be no doubt that this is just the kind of narrative which would have held William and Dorothy, of Grasmere, spell-bound. ...

"Ivanhoe," in the *Winnipeg Tribune*, November 30, 1922. By permission of the *Winnipeg Tribune*.

This is an attractive-looking volume, issued by the well known Toronto firm of publishers. It is rather romantically and fancifully illustrated by C. U. Manly, A.R.C.A. ... The author's powers of observation and memory must be highly developed. He presents almost photographic pictures of what he saw and experienced. His literary style is clear and concise.

W.E.M., *Dalhousie Review*, II (1922-3), 528. By permission of *Dalhousie Review*.

... I do not know of a more vivid or authentic description of inland Canadian weather. There is combined the naturalist's scientific accuracy and attention to detail with the poet's interpretative affection. The chapter on "Snow" with its remarkable study of snow shapes and flake movement is a good illustration of the writer as naturalist, and the almost mystic quality of "Fog" is one of many evidences of the poet. ... Although there are a few rhetorical paragraphs which seem to strain somewhat for effect, and two or three expressions which strike one as a

bit careless, the book is one of the rare prose works written
in Canada which do not need the indulgence of the special
domestic Canadian standard of style.

Canadian Forum, May 1923, 248-250 (unsigned). By permission of
Canadian Forum.

. . . Though the child of a Swedish father and a Scottish
mother, he is a Canadian in sympathies and outlook, and
his books are autochthonous to a degree seldom attained
by native authors. As authentic and lively descriptions of
local phenomena, they belong to the same general class as
Mrs. Jameson's *Winter Studies and Summer Rambles* and
Mrs. Moodie's *Roughing it in the Bush*. Such attempts to
reproduce local color and to transmit atmosphere through
the medium of words are rarer than one might expect. In
our generation Peter McArthur's *In Pastures Green* and
Janey Canuck's *Open Trails* and *Seeds of Pine*, being readable records of Canadian conditions and ways, embody
valuable and entertaining material, but many sections of
the country have yet had no scribe to delineate and interpret them. . . . So graphically does Mr. Grove describe the
roads, the woods, the farms and the sky-signs indicating the
kind of weather he expects, that one is drawn into the
cutter and shares with the driver his anxiety about being
able to reach his destination without accident. There were
accidents. Every trip was an adventure, and getting Mr.
Grove safely home every week becomes a positive nerve-
strain on the reader. The author's capacity for holding
prisoner the reader's imagination is sufficient justification
for the book; that he has a frank, free style, well under
command, and that he conveys subtly an understanding of
the lives of the inhabitants, is in the nature of a bonus.

The presentation and interpretation of the human part
of his environment, though sure, is a secondary matter.
His main concern is meteorological: he has theories as to
when and why snow falls, and drifts into certain shapes;
he has a novel and scientific explanation of fogs. He loves

a storm. It may mean that he risks freezing to death, but it gives him something to look at, and think about. Never is he so happy as when he sits behind those horses deducing from the direction of the wind and the aspect of the sky the exact nature of the natural calamity that is about to overtake him. It has been said that the test of a writer is his ability to take for subject "nothing but the weather," and turn out an original and interesting paragraph upon it. By this criterion Mr. Grove is in a class by himself, for he has made a whole book of it—undoubtedly original, and on the side of "interest" nothing short of absorbing. I would not for a great deal have missed these rides he, by his skill, has allowed me to share.

"Candide," *Saturday Night*, January 3, 1925. By permission of *Saturday Night*.

The Turn of the Year (1923)

. . . There are two things that have mightily impressed me in Mr. Grove's books, his Wordsworthian appreciation of the minute life of Nature and his interpretation of the kinship of man with Nature. In *The Turn of the Year,* we see through his eyes the color and glory, the grayness and the melancholy as spring changes into summer and summer into fall; and against this prairie background we see various human beings engaged in the struggle of pioneering life. . . .

"Ivanhoe," in the *Winnipeg Tribune,* December 4, 1923, By permission of the *Winnipeg Tribune.*

. . . No detail of each season's movements escapes his lynx-eyes which are the eyes of his heart. But I cannot help thinking that some day he will revise these essays, cutting without maiming—especially certain idioms and colloquial phrases—and polishing lengthy passages into terseness. . . .

"The Bookman," A Reader's Notes, *Manitoba Free Press,* December 19, 1923. By permission of the *Winnipeg Free Press.*

The Turn of the Year gives a hint of subtleties of emotion and the joy of living which the human drama of the prairie may develop in its next act. If Canadian criticism was not already sprinkled over with pompous analogies, we might call Mr. Grove a Manitoba Thoreau. He knows equally well his Darwin and his Burroughs; but he is not a replica nor an imitation. He differs from others who have written about nature in his focus of interest. Birds are not his chief interest, nor animals, nor plants, though he may write of them all in turn. The larger aspects of nature fascinate him—forests as such, marshes, grass-plains, the battling of the seasons. Perhaps he is unique in his delight in the varied phenomena which we usually throw together in the one word, weather. These he observes with an understanding and delicacy that makes us conscious of inexcusable obtuseness in ourselves. . . .

"A.L.S.,"in *The Canadian Student,* January, 1924. By permission of the Student Christian Movement of Canada.

It is probably quite misleading to say that Mr. Grove is a naturalist and meteorologist, with the pathetic fallacy as his creed, but such is the impression left by both his published books. This second one, with its setting still in northern Manitoba, marks, I think, a distinct advance on the first. The framework is practically the same, a series of essays bound loosely together by a seasonal sequence, still connected, but much less definitely, with a series of road trips. Within this seasonal framework there are three charming little vignettes, glimpses at the rural spring, summer and autumn of two simple lives; the second sketch quite Hamsunesque, the third somewhat sentimental, but not the less true. The interpretative poetry, the minute and scientific observation of *Over Prairie Trails*, strike one just as impressively in this book, and the same remarkable sense of word values. Mr. Grove seems to rely more on the actual pictorial content of the individual word than on structure, and the closeness of application which this

method requires from the reader draws attention inevitably to any unevenness in style, as does probably, too, the
very distinction of the writer's general style. Such unevenness, of rather frequent occurrence in the other book, is
much less evident in *The Turn of the Year*. The moody
bitterness, too, which expected no understanding appreciation from us, and announced this lack of expectation, is
noticeably absent. There are still two criticisms which
will probably be made. The author is a born educationist,
and cannot help teaching sometimes when we are not
anxious to be taught. The second ground for objection
may arise partly from this, partly from the intensity of
Mr. Grove's absorption in the details of nature as well as
in its general effects. Whatever be the cause, there is in
places a fatiguing minuteness of sustained description
which calls for dilution with incident, and which conveys,
rightly or wrongly, an impression of repetition. It is this
that helps to make the vignettes, the sower, the harvester,
the lost calf, so welcome. Still, as long as Mr. Grove can
give us such epics of movements in the heavens as in the
latter part of "Woods in June," we can gladly forgive him
his explanation of why the lower parts of horizon clouds
are straight, and we shall even read through his botanical
enumerations.

Canadian Forum, January 1924, 152-154 (unsigned) By permission of
Canadian Forum.

This title suggests *At the Turn of the Year* by Fiona
Macleod, and the Canadian book is worthy of comparison
with the latter. Fiona Macleod's work includes with nature
an interest in folklore and the mythical, while that of Mr.
Grove is mainly description of nature with a human interest thrown in.

These glimpses of people through the pages of *The
Turn of the Year* are so attractive that one wishes that this
second book of Mr. Grove's had been mainly about people
with a little nature interest thrown in. One feels he knows

how to tell a story as few can. Those sketches of the Icelander, and of John and Ellen for instance: there is a glory and glow about the pictures; there is strength and character in the composition.

In that first splendid story, *Over Prairie Trails,* every aspect of nature described was necessary to the progress of the narrative. The sky, the air, the ground were scanned anxiously, for on them as well as on the strength and sagacity of his horses, and his own fortitude and ingenuity, depended the success of his long prairie drives. But in this second book there is no such good reason for the somewhat prolix descriptions of weather conditions. The author has yielded to his own intense interest in them. These descriptions are not "meaningless"; they are real, vivid, beautifully done; but whereas in *Over Prairie Trails* they contribute their share to drama and suspense, in *The Turn of the Year* they must depend largely upon their own intrinsic value for interest.

One can hardly speak too highly of Mr. Grove as a writer, nor hope too much—and we do hope he will act on our suggestion.

The Library Table, January 1924, 219 (unsigned).

In *The Turn of the Year,* Mr. Grove, with all the charm and pithiness characteristic of *Over Prairie Trails,* shows much greater versatility as he reconstructs the advent of the season of profusion, the diverse and multitudinous incidents of the full blooming, and the strenuous battle in which summer perishes amidst the ruins of its glory. During July and August the author took charge of a country school, this time twenty-five miles north of his wife's residence, and in considerable discomfort put the tiny institution into working shape.

Valuable as that work must have been, Mr. Grove keeps his professional toils in the background, and presents the hail and the rain, and development of thunder-storms and the heart-breaking drought that discourages the pioneer farmer. In brief, illuminating sketches, he gives us pictures of the people at work, and an insight into the motives that impel them to action and control their destinies. The weekly bicycle rides home are not in themselves as engrossing as were the winter drives, but there was more to see, particularly in the way of human activity, and Mr. Grove may be counted upon always to see, and reproduce, those details that are colorful and significant. As Mr. Arthur L. Phelps aptly says in his "Foreword": "It is a little unfair to Mr. Grove to say he is a nature writer. He is more than that. In his work nature is seldom, even momentarily, viewed apart from humanity. As it rains, there is a man watching the rain. As the seasons operate man is seen accommodating himself." I only wish to add that the two books are really one work in two volumes, and that they should be read as one, in the order of publication.

"Candide," *Saturday Night*, January 3, 1925. By permission of *Saturday Night*.

Settlers of the Marsh (1925)

It is a most welcome sign in the new Canadian fiction that it reveals no effort to please the reader but rather a determination on the part of the author to be true to his own standard, to say what he set out to say, and to avoid all meretricious paths to popularity. That is the only way any young nation can build up its literature, whether in the realm of fiction, *belles lettres*, or verse. *Wild Geese*, which I reviewed the other day, was a notable case in point. This week I have read two other outstanding examples, each highly meritorious in its own way.

Settlers of the Marsh, by Frederick Philip Grove, is the more serious of these two books. It is a story of life in a small Swedish farming settlement in the Northwest—or more properly the story of Niels Lindstedt, a young Swedish immigrant. He falls in love with the quiet, self-contained daughter of a farmer, but she will not marry him, because of the tragedy of her own mother's married life. He turns to another and a grosser passion, marries a worthless woman, stands for a time in danger of mental and moral destruction, and only escapes by taking the law into his own hands. The book closes on a note of expiation and a prospect of peace through the regenerating influence of love.

It is a big theme—at times it seems a tremendous theme. Mr. Grove has handled it with fearlessness and candour. Some will feel he has been too frank, but there is about this frankness a stark directness and a grim sincerity that rob it of all offensiveness. Hand in hand with the man's fight goes on the unceasing struggle between man and nature, between the pioneer and the land. With masterly simplicity Mr. Grove sets this forth, and indicates the relation between the two. His understanding of the influence of the primitive pioneer life upon human nature is deep, and he has utilised it to enable his readers to grasp the full force of the tragedy he depicts. His style is easy. He handles dramatic situations with a firm hand, and he has a keen sense of proportion and of emotional values. This is no book for children to read. But adults will find in it a conscientious and powerful study of the fight between the two extremes of human nature in the same man. Its strength is unchallengeable. Its sincerity is obvious. Its truth will be evident to those who read it without prejudice and with the desire to understand. It is essentially a big thing to have done, and I regard it as an important contribution to contemporary fiction in the English-speaking world.

The Montreal Daily Star, October 31, 1925. By permission of *The Montreal Star*.

The first full dress novel by Mr. Grove will be read with sympathetic interest all over Canada and more particularly by the people of this province in which Mr. Grove has passed so much of his life. The story, which finds its setting in a Swedish settlement of Manitoba, gives evidence of careful work, and there are passages of graphic writing that exhibit Mr. Grove's not inconsiderable power at its height. It is, therefore, with the more regret that we record profound disappointment at the result. The ambitious theme requires a deftness of touch and a certainty of feeling which only a great master could approach. Mr. Grove's treatment of the subject falls far short of what he needed.

The central character of the story, Niels Lindstedt, falls in love with a simple girl, Ellen Amundsen, who, however, refuses to marry, for she has seen her mother slowly done to death by the brutish lust of her father. This story she tells Niels in language which falls ineptly from the tongue of a Swedish girl, brought up without schooling on a lonely farm—"An abyss opened as I lay there. The vile, jesting jocular urging of it; the words he used to that skeleton and ghost of a woman . . . I was tempted to betray that I heard. Shame held me back."

Such unnatural dialogue would not be so serious a blemish—there are serfs and varlets in the Waverley Novels who speak with a strangely fluent brilliance—were it not that the falsity spreads into the characters themselves.

Rejected by Ellen, Niels falls in with Mrs. Vogel, a notorious character in the district, known as the "gay widow," who seduces him. To her unbounded amazement, as well as to the reader's, he insists upon marriage, and the story moves swiftly on to its conclusion.

Niels can neither see for himself what his wife is, nor can he understand the hints hurled at him from all sides. He is astonished to find his home ostracized, and after a long period of growing misery, he murders his wife who has reverted to her dissolute habits of life.

The utter distortion of the story is responsible for its collapse. Mr. Grove first presents Mrs. Vogel, before her marriage with Niels, accepted and honored by the respectably married women of the district. He then sends her to

Coventry. The inconsistency of woman is supposed to be their proudest privilege, but here is one instance in which they stand as steadfast as the rock of Gibraltar. They will not condone immorality. That is simply not done, and in making his womenfolk do it, Mr. Grove, not for the only time in his story, forces his characters ruthlessly to follow his story, instead of making the story flow naturally from them.

No emphasis need be laid on the simplicity of Niels, which passes all reasonable understanding. Nor need anything be said of the happy ending roughly tacked on after Niels has served his term in prison. It is useless also to complain of the diffusion of interest over too wide a group of characters. Complaint on these counts is to strain at the gnat after swallowing the camel.

Mr. Grove has suffered the fate of Icarus, whose wings of wax availed him not when put to too severe a test. In more modest efforts there is hope of a happier flight of the author's powers.

G. V. Ferguson, "A Prairie Story," *Manitoba Free Press*, Winnipeg, November 2, 1925. By permission of the *Winnipeg Free Press*.

Frederick Philip Grove's *Settlers of the Marsh* suggests in one aspect, and one only, an instant comparison with Martha Ostenso's *Wild Geese*. So similar is the locale that the "Yellow Post" of *Wild Geese* might be the "Minor" of *Settlers of the Marsh* in the north country of Manitoba in the wooded area. It is tempting to compare (which would involve contrast at every point) the two novels further. Mr. Grove's plot is, though melodramatic enough, stated baldly, not so well adapted to the movies as is Miss Ostenso's. I must say this, I do not think that the story of *Settlers of the Marsh* is linked so inevitably, bound so closely to the locality, that rough pioneering neighborhood where its action takes place, as is that of *Wild Geese*. Niel's catastrophe is one that might have happened to him with a good deal more likelihood in a town or city. I do not find Mrs. Vogel's presence in the marsh neighborhood quite convincing.

Yet Niels Lindstedt, the protagonist of the action, is a notable creation. His denseness to certain implications is not stupidity, does honor rather to his innate goodness. He acts at the crisis of his life as one would expect him to act. He is drawn with skill—is consistent, is real. So, also, is Ellen Amundsen. Her tragedy is no less grievous than his end, all so needless but perfectly credible. She is inhibited —Freud penetrates Canada—by contact with the sordid in her parents' married life. That she should let Niels go off after she has told him why she can never marry, without a hint that perhaps she may come to change her mind, is just another instance of the perversity of fate that makes a life's happiness turn upon a trifling action or failure to act.

Fate plays with Niels and Ellen in the spirit of Thomas Hardy's relentlessness.

Mr. Francis Dickie will have to retract his nonsensical statement that his novel *Roads of Desire* is the only published Canadian novel to which the word realism, as he understands it, can be applied. For *Settlers of the Marsh* quite falls within his postulates of the realistic novel as a work in which "the sex motive takes its proper place and proportion as the great ground rhythm of the universe." This despite the close: "An hour or so later they rise and walk home through the dust. They do not kiss. Their lips have not touched. But their arms rest in each other's: their fingers are intertwined. As they go, a vision arises between them shared by both."

The outstanding distinction of *Settlers of the Marsh* is its style, simple but forceful. Occasionally one detects the conscious will. It is one of the concerns of the writer to achieve the art that conceals art. That he does not always succeed is axiomatic. I have nothing but praise for Mr.

Grove's writing. It is obvious that one does not compare him with Ralph Connor, but with, shall one say, Sherwood Anderson. One can but measure him in his art against the greater realists who picture man, "an immemorially suffering figure against an unrelieved background of ruthless and tragic nature." Thus Mr. Dickie! But is he quite exact? *Settlers of the Marsh* has a happy ending. I will maintain that that doesn't exclude it from being a realistic novel. For the happiness is bought with a price. It is a glad and confident future that Niels and Ellen face because they have known grief and frustration in the past. Certainly a notable novel *Settlers of the Marsh*! A first novel, it is mature in thought, well-constructed. It has distinction in style and a theme that is real, not just contrived.

Austin Bothwell, "A Canadian Bookshelf," in *Saskatoon Phoenix*, November 14, 1925. By permission of the *Star-Phoenix*.

Mr. Grove's first novel is an extremely grim and powerful realistic study of life among the Scandinavian settlers of the Canadian prairies. . . . It is a brutally virile, uncompromising book, obviously not suitable for those who like their fiction gay, smart and shallow, but well worth comparison with the best of Mr. Knopf's imported Norsemen.

New York Sun, November 14, 1925 (unsigned).

Of the many Canadian novels published this season, two at least have such merit, not to say genius, that they will take their places in our national literature. These novels are *Wild Geese* by Miss Martha Ostenso . . . and *Settlers of the Marsh* by Frederick Philip Grove. . . . We might call these stories sister and brother, for both are realistic studies of foreign-born settlement life in Manitoba. They do for our back country districts what *Maria Chapdelaine* did for the pioneering region in northern Quebec; like Louis Hémon's famous story, they are full of atmosphere, and the supreme motif in each is love of the soil. They are both sombre in tone, in this respect also resembling the French-Canadian story, and, again, both are written in a style of stark directness and simplicity. . . .

W. T. Allison, *The Winnipeg Tribune* Magazine, November 21, 1925, 13. By permission of *The Winnipeg Tribune*.

In *Settlers of the Marsh* Frederick Philip Grove gives us a picture of farm life, during the free pioneering stage, in a mostly Scandinavian settlement. Life, character, customs, everything is "facts"—facts more crude than romantic.

Mr. Grove's book is not to be recommended for too young people. It is not immoral—far from it—but there is, here and there, some quite plain talk. Its wholesome lesson might affect unripe minds in the same way it affected the mind of Ellen Amundsen (the main character of the story, second only to Niels Lindstedt, its real hero). Ellen, having seen part of the tragic, even criminal, side of motherhood on a homestead, refused to marry Niels. He married a low creature, who drove him mad, and he had a taste of a Canadian penitentiary. Finally. . . . But the merit of this novel is not so much in the tale. It is found in the true painting of pioneer life in a bush country, with full details of the work it entails—too many, perhaps, in the first part of the book. It is found, too, in a fairly accurate and penetrating analysis of the debasing influence of a sensual and vindictive woman over a good and strong man.

Mr. F. P. Grove has certainly the marks of a gifted writer who knows how to curb his imagination to let facts, real facts, predominate.

George Bugnet, *Canadian Author and Bookman*, VII, December 1925, 203. By permission of The Canadian Authors Association.

Here is a book out of the Great West of Canada which suggests things profound and enduring, whose body of artistic purpose charges through the usual sentimental lithographs and shows them for what they are—the mere coloured paper of the circus ring. Artistically not so delicately satisfying, yet with a more aggressive vitality, this book comes off the prairies as *Maria Chapdelaine* came out of the Quebec woods. It is the tale of Niels, a Swedish immigrant who goes into serfdom to the land bound by a beautiful dream. Two women and the land are Niels' life. One of the women is Ellen, the bachelor girl of the prairie settlement; the other is Mrs. Vogel, the prostitute of the community. The story is in reality a simple one. The action is internal and significant.

The vitality of the writing comes from the author's power to create setting, situation and character by strokes swift, simple, and effective. Niels and Mrs. Vogel are so vitally present to the reader that one notes with exasperation certain shortcomings of Grove in the presentation of them; the minor and supporting folk of the community are physically inescapable. In similar physical fashion the prairie is made to underlie all the activities of the book. The prairie settlement concerned stretches out under the eye with houses in perspective and towns on the horizon. But it is when setting and characterization are together involved to create a particular scene or situation that Mr. Grove's power most manifests itself. The crucial clash between Niels and his wife, the happenings of the evening and night of the murder, constitute themselves unforgettable scenes which bother the memory. One goes to the great novelist or to life itself in order to suggest that to which they approximate.

In matter of sex the book does not preserve the usual Anglo-Saxon delicacies. It may be the cleaner and more sincere for that. Certainly there is no unwholesomeness in it, and its ending, an inevitable outworking of the characterization, though not gayly happy, is quietly beautiful.

Those who possess a shelf for Hardy and Hamsun and certain others, because he is of their kind, will place Grove on that shelf.

As a novel, *Settlers of the Marsh* is not without superficial flaws. But its people are alive. This uncanny power of the book to make people and landscape physically intrusively real, its sincerity, penetration and straightforward good writing place it at once in the ranks of the significant contemporary fiction. That settlement and those men and women are embarrassingly real, with a reality against which the hearty Canadian will desire to defend himself.

Arthur L. Phelps, *Saturday Night*, December 5, 1925. By permission of *Saturday Night*.

. . . The frontier life of primitive loves and hates and ambitions is convincingly visualized. Mr. Grove evidently knows from personal observation, if not from personal experience, the laborious life of the settlers of the far northern wildernesses, and their rude habitats, even as Louis Hémon knew the country and people around Lake St. John. Introspection is inevitable in these forests and marsh solitudes and human longings and passions denied normal outlet seize the more avidly upon whatever opening presents itself. . . .

As a study of pioneer wilderness life the novel is strongly convincing. As a story, however, remembering Hugh Walpole's dictum that a novel must first be "a good story," secondly "a good story"—it is much less so. At least it was to us.

Boston Evening Transcript, December 23, 1925, 6.

. . . There are two tremendous scenes in the book and a multitude of intensely vivid little pictures of all sorts; there is detailed, subtle characterization and the presentation of many folk who appear physically alive to us and whom we might wish to know; there is presentation of a prairie settlement rising out of the gumbo and becoming articulated into Canadian life. Under all, upholding all, is the prairie landscape; overall, as a presence, is the prairie sky at night and by day. This vivid, compelling intensity of the book is blurred and offset from time to time by what appear to be tricks of style—the spendthrift use of dots suggesting that anything but the prolific linotype would have run out of periods by the end of the first chapter; a nervous haste destroying the reader's desire for leisure as he reads; the apparent lack of verisimilitude in the speech of certain characters; in one or two places an inartistic amount of detail in handling the sex elements of the book; and a rather hurried ending. . . .

Mr. Grove's knowledge is so thorough, his style so economical and effective, that his literary product becomes one of those inescapable things carrying with it an undeniable challenge to our attention. One is tempted to the statement that no pen at work in Canada suggests the capacity, not primarily to tell a story, but to interpret the actuality of Western prairie life in the making, as does the pen of Frederick Philip Grove; no one is creating as Grove is creating it the kind of literature to which one goes in order to get the sense of life, of men and women alive body and soul, of landscape under foot and eye. With this book, *Settlers of the Marsh,* Canada makes a contribution to contemporary world fiction.

A. L. Phelps, *The Saturday Review of Literature,* January 30, 1926, 529. (This review had appeared earlier in the *Manitoba Free Press,* December 7, 1925.) By permission of the *Winnipeg Free Press.*

. . . In Frederick Philip Grove's *Settlers of the Marsh,* the surroundings are very similar to those in *Wild Geese* and the scene is definitely fixed in our West. It could be written only by one with a long and intimate knowledge of pioneering, with unusual powers of analysis, and with a highly developed sense of the dramatic.

Professor Arthur Phelps of Winnipeg says that the book sends one at once to Thomas Hardy for a basis of comparison. How much Grove has in common with the novelist of Wessex will be immediately recognized by admirers of the genius of the latter. *Settlers of the Marsh,* in the opinion

of Professor Phelps, "fuses with the universal and out of
Manitoba landscape creates spiritual territory of the soul."
This is high commendation, but it is warranted.

Willisons Monthly, February 1926, 342 (unsigned).

It is curious that two of the best novels dealing with the
western prairie life should have come from the pens of
writers of Scandinavian origin. Frederick Philip Grove's
Settlers of the Marsh, published by the Ryerson Press, is
no less powerful a story than Martha Ostenso's *Wild
Geese*, and there is a marked similarity in general design
and treatment of their respective tales. Again we touch the
strenuous life of those settlers, Scandinavian, German, Icelandic and other races, who built homes on the outer
fringes of the earlier settlements. . . .

I find in him the same keen observing mind that I find
in Thoreau, in Richard Jefferies, and Burroughs. I feel
quite sure that Mr. Grove knows his *Walden* well, that he
is familiar with old Gilbert White of Selborne, and W. H.
Hudson. And if he has not read E. L. Grant Watson's
English Country I venture to commend it to his notice as
a book after his own heart. No one has more finely and
delicately sketched the thousand and one little things that
mark the change of the seasons in those great spaces of the
west. He has pictured in a way most rare, and most perceiv-
ing, the yielding of that long harsh winter to the oncoming
spring. In late March he marks, when the welcome cawing
of the crow is heard, the "strange, new quality in the feel
of the air." John Burroughs himself never noted with more
sympathy and truth the movement of that pulsing and
varied bird-life of the early spring.

But Mr. Grove has not omitted *Homo sapiens* in his wide
studies, and of those rugged and toiling settlers, who have
brought the virgin prairie under the dominion of the
plough, he writes in his last book with both power and
insight. Nearly always he uses the fit word. Why, I wonder,

does he employ the old seventeenth century spelling of
"squalour" and "pallour?" . . .

"M," *The Ottawa Journal*, February 20, 1926. By permission of *The
Ottawa Journal*.

Frederick Philip Grove is one of the most promising Canadian authors whose writings have begun to appear in the
last few years. . . . In no other author can one get a more
vivid pictorial representation of the phenomena of earth
and sky on the prairies than in these two volumes.

Now Mr. Grove has published a novel over which he
has worked for years. *Settlers of the Marsh* is one of the
great novels of the new school of realism in Canadian
fiction. Those who have read Laura Goodman Salverson's
prose epic, *The Viking Heart*, will find in *Settlers of the
Marsh* the same elemental grandeur, the same skilful portrayal of human character. This new novel is a profound
artistic treatment of sexual love. The plot traces the far-
reaching evil of love on a wrong basis. Because of the
sordid selfishness of her father in his conjugal relations, the
heroine decides that she will accept no lover unless he is
willing to put love on a purely spiritual basis. This drives
the hero to love on the merely physical plane and to
marriage with a woman who has made a profession of love
on that plane. The logic with which the effect on these
three characters in the story is represented is worthy of the
highest praise. Not only is the plot thus the essential outcome of the influence of the characters on each other and
of the interaction of character and environment, but the
moods of nature and the seasons of the year are har-
monized or contrasted with the dramatic situations in so
consummately artistic a manner as to recall the genius of
Thomas Hardy. It is largely because of this poetic treatment of environment in relation to situation that no
reader is ever likely to forget the scene in which the
heroine demanded love on a purely spiritual basis, or that
in which, after the tragedy of merely physical love, she

offered herself to the same lover on a proper human basis.
We look forward to more novels by the same author.

V. B. Rhodenizer, *Book Parlance*, March 1926, 20.

A Search for America (1927)

Unless I am badly mistaken, *A Search for America* is one
of the most important books that has been published in
Canada by a Canadian for some years. . . .

. . . Consciously or unconsciously, most Canadian book
reviewers make allowance for a Canadian book. I have been
known to make allowances in this way myself. The result
is that a Canadian book is often praised because, by Canadian standards, it stacks up well with its fellows. But apply
a universal standard to Canadian books, and it has to be
confessed that most of them fail to merit being described as
distinctive. Compare, for example, the work of leading
women novelists of England, United States and Canada.
What is the result? The result is that Canada is nowhere.
(I have not read *Jalna*.) Compare the best biographies and
autobiographies of the same countries—and the same result
is apparent.

But it is in such company and by such standards that *A
Search for America* can hold its own. In fact, the first book
to which it may aptly be compared is Ludwig Lewisohn's
Upstream. Now *Upstream* is one of the most distinguished
autobiographies of recent years, and it is also a profound
and moving criticism of life—American life. *A Search for
America* is an autobiography. It, too, is a criticism of
American life. It has not the poignant beauty of *Upstream*,
nor quite its inner significance, but, nevertheless, it bears
comparison and emerges from that comparison a fine up-
standing book of great interest and considerable beauty.

. . . The narrative is full of absorbing incidents and
equally absorbing speculations. There is also some excellent character drawing. And it is all written in a limpid

and flowing style. An author's note says that *A Search for America* has been written and rewritten eight times during the last thirty-two years. For my part I can well believe it. It bears signs of having been composed with great care and mature thought. It is as interesting as any work of the imagination and might, with little difficulty, have been transformed into a striking novel. Had this been done, one of the greatest Canadian novels so far would now be on the bookstands. As it is, *A Search for America* will long remain one of the outstanding human documents from the pen of a Canadian writer.

E. W. Harrold, *The Ottawa Citizen*, November 26, 1927 By permission of *The Ottawa Citizen*.

. . . Nearly two years ago we read Mr. Grove's novel, *Settlers of the Marsh*, and were impressed with the strength and fidelity of his work. We followed it up by reading two small volumes of his essays. Here, too, we noted the soul of a great artist and of a great lover of nature. *Settlers of the Marsh* offended the unco guid of Manitoba, and was, we understand, banned from the public library of Winnipeg. Those responsible for such action may have had the sincerity of Comstock; they had, in intensified form, his narrowness of vision. The book, though frank in regard to sexual matters, perhaps unwisely frank, was absolutely free from salacity.

The censoring—none the less effective for being unofficial—was a cruel blow to a Canadian author of distinction. It might have been well to have directed the attention of those self-constituted guardians of the public conscience to the words of that sane old Hebrew philosopher, Ecclesiastes, who implored his people, "Be not righteous over much; neither make thyself over wise." Sturdy old Milton himself didn't believe much in these gentlemen who compel conformity with their standards on literary matters, and remarked pungently of one such, "I have his own hand for his arrogance; who shall warrant me for his judgment?"

The sale of Mr. Grove's last novel must have been a deep disappointment. We shall be surprised if *A Search for America* shares a similar fate. Even the most squeamish of readers will find nothing here to offend his fastidious taste, and all will find the sincere and forceful record of one who passed through many evil adventures and emerged unscathed, still captain of his soul. For this book is unquestionably the story of Mr. Grove's own early life on this continent. Philip Branden tells the story, but so stark and sincere a record of life is not spun from the imagination. Here is a voice which speaks authoritatively of things done, and seen, and heard by the speaker, and his message carries conviction.

"M," *The Ottawa Journal*, November 26, 1927. By permission of *The Ottawa Journal*.

A great book, a vital and compelling one, Mr. Grove's narrative dramatizes the longings of the immigrant for realization of an ideal of fair play and opportunity and the spirit of brotherhood; his desire to be assimilated; his handicaps and his trials; and some suggestions for his betterment to the end of relieving the country from the dangers of a floating population.

The story is of a spiritual rather than a geographical quest. Soul-moulding experiences—some of them bitter enough—have gone to the making of the book, which excels in the clarity and profundity with which the subject is treated. By presenting his material in the form of a novel, he will increase the number of his readers, but cannot disguise the deep purpose underlying the work: on the contrary, the fictional dress lends his facts the emphasis of personal, concrete exemplification. With every line carrying conviction, and being written in the first person, there is not so much danger of the reader disbelieving in the conditions described as that he will too readily assume each incident to be a literal transcription from the author's life. . . .

W. A. Deacon, *Saturday Night*, December 3, 1927. By permission of *Saturday Night*.

To many readers Frederick Philip Grove's book will be a revelation. Dealing ostensibly with a quest for the spiritual essence of America, it is in reality an Odyssey of the soul and the quest resolves itself into introspection and finally into acceptance.

We have in the pages a spiritual cosmos with the gradual and painful metamorphoses that are incidental to evolution. Phil Branden tasted bitter waters; he was athirst and, like many more, received the sponge dipped in vinegar; yet in the relation of his progress we catch a glimpse of the influences that, intrinsically transient and without seeming significance, shape and mould the destiny of the individual. . . .

It is a pleasure to praise this book unreservedly. Although it is written from an unusual angle it applies "mutatis mutandis" to the immigrant in general and it throws into high relief the varying phases and processes of orientation as concerned with the newcomer in America. For this reason the book is vital and provocative of thought and the generally high level of prose—the sincerity of the whole—mark it as a book that should be read—and read widely—by all those who are interested in vital experiences.

T. D. Rimmer, *The Canadian Author and Bookman*, January 1928. By permission of the Canadian Authors Association

In *A Search for America*, Mr. Frederick Philip Grove has written the story of a young man of education who came to this land as an immigrant, who lived as best he could from day to day, who wandered over much of the United States and about all of Canada, finally to settle in the

Dominion. Unpretentious in every way, the narrative is one that holds the mind of the reader, first, because the writer had the ability to observe, and secondly, because he thought deeply on all that he saw and on all that he experienced.

One reads from time to time of the man of good family and careful upbringing who is found working as a dishwasher. Grove (or, as he calls himself, "Branden"), was glad to get such a position when his money gave out, and to work at it faithfully until something better offered. He worked in mills; as a canvasser for books; as a harvest hand; as a farmhand. From time to time the desire merely to rove overcame him, when he dropped whatever he was engaged on and took to the open road. Then his pages are such as would have delighted Stevenson himself, although they are never worked up to the same degree of artistry that Stevenson demanded in the accounts of his own wanderings. On the other hand, the author of *Travels with a Donkey* and *An Inland Voyage* could not have done Grove's account of riding under trains to get to the wheat country, for the reason he could never have done such a thing himself, or even have imagined doing it.

Yet neither description nor narration nor observation nor reflection is the core and kernel of *A Search for America*. Mr. Grove (alias "Branden") was impelled by a motive. He wanted to discover America, to see it as the immigrant sees it, feel it as the immigrant feels it. Mr. Grove disclaims any lesson in the book for Americans, whether they dwell north or south of the line dividing Canada and the United States. Nevertheless, there is a lesson. But it does not intrude.

As we queried above: Why is it that not more books come out of Canada? *A Search for America* brings the sudden realization that there is material as rich, and there must be authors quite as capable, as south of the border. And as a piece of bookwork, especially in the manner of printing, the volume before us proves that there are good

Canadian publishers. It is time that Canadian literature became something more imposing and more important than what some one once called it—"a mere bud on the tree of the great Anglo-Saxon tradition."

The New York Times Book Supplement, January 15, 1928 (unsigned), © 1928 by The New York Times Company. Reprinted by permission.

This is the record of a search for a far country which has no geographical delimitations, a land not bounded by any of the Seven Seas or surveyed frontiers, and it may be that the America of this search might be found in Astrakhan or Zanzibar, or indeed any part of the world's surface. And yet this may need some qualification, for Branden, the Columbus of the story, in his quest for some soil in which he could take root and grow, is seeking an ideal which, in his case, could be most richly fulfilled only on this continent. The history of the Americas is largely a record of the immigrant and his struggles with a new environment, and this account of the newcomer during the process of adaptation deals with this theme so adequately, with so much insight, that the book might fairly be described as the epic of the immigrant.

This is a book that defies classification. It breaks with nearly all literary tradition, except perhaps the tradition that all work which has elements of greatness must break with the established rules. It is not fiction, neither is it history, philosophy, or biography, and yet at the same time it is all of these. It is, in my estimation, one of a few really distinguished literary works that have been produced in this country. Here is no heady best-seller, but a vintage which will improve with keeping.

J. F. White, The Canadian Forum, March 1928, 576-7. By permission of Canadian Forum.

Autobiographical novels seldom maintain so even a level of truthfulness, consistency and restraint as that followed throughout this story of several years' wandering in the author's early lifetime. . . . It is a stout book (448 pages stout), unusual for the purity of its style, for its sober thoughtfulness, for the unquestionable worth of its purpose and ideas.

Saturday Review of Literature, April 21, 1928 (unsigned). By permission of *Saturday Review*.

Since the days of Columbus—and possibly the Vikings—America has been "discovered" over and over again by succeeding generations of explorers and immigrants, and the continued story of this succession of adventurous exploits still retains in many of its later chapters all the romantic charm of its prolog. An impressive example of such captivating sequels is *A Search for America*. . . . As its subtitle proclaims, this book is "the Odyssey of an immigrant." It is not so truly, as its publishers suggest elsewhere, "the story of the coming of the European."

In some measure, to be sure, this book may be presumed to tell a typical story of immigrants in general, their hopes, disappointments and disillusionments; their search for work, their failures and successes. In the main, however, *A Search for America* is too thoroughly individualized an autobiographical tale to be regarded as a composite story of "the European's" arrival. It is rather a unique record of one particular European's finally successful search, not merely for work and a home in America, but also for the embodiments of America's distinctive ideals. . . .

Taken as a whole, this vividly realistic account of a gifted young man's struggle to adapt himself to a strange environment and his later philosophical quest for the "Abraham Lincoln" of America has a youthful vitality that makes it timely regardless of the calendar.

The Springfield Republican, April 24, 1928, 10 (unsigned).

. . . The winning of the *Atlantic Monthly* prize by Mazo de la Roche's *Jalna* will probably turn out to be a less significant event than the appearance of Frederick Philip

Grove's *A Search for America*, which is soon to be published also in Great Britain and the United States. Grove, a man of 57, of Swedish-Scottish parentage, and a graduate of a Swedish university, migrated to Canada in 1894; and after a childhood spent in travel and an atmosphere of luxury settled down as a farm-hand in Manitoba, where his chief interests were writing and teaching the children of the foreign-born. Ultimately he became a high school principal in the village of Rapid City, where he still lives. He is six feet two inches in height, of commanding personality, and, except for his eyes, his looks betray little of the thirty years of poverty, hardship, illness and disappointment he has endured.

His first books to be published, entitled *Over Prairie Trails* and *The Turn of the Year* (1922, 1923), are collections of splendidly firm descriptive essays that had been written in 1917 and 1919 respectively. *Settlers of the Marsh*, a grim novel, was under construction from 1902 till 1917. On its publication in 1925, its circulation was hindered by its being banned by the Winnipeg Public Library. The acclaim that greeted *A Search for America* has sent all three of the former books into new editions; and another novel, *Our Daily Bread*, which the author describes as "unrelieved tragedy," is to be published in New York next autumn. Grove's present popularity has put him above the danger line for his own daily bread.

A Search for America, written in 1894-95, when the bitterness of his struggles as an immigrant was still fresh upon him, takes the form of a novel, but is almost pure autobiography. It tells of the arrival of the cultured European youth in Toronto, where the only job he could get was that of a busboy in a cheap restaurant. From that he rose to be a waiter, and with a goodly accumulation of tips sought New York—the "America" of his dreams, the land of potential Lincolns, of freedom, opportunity, and fair play. Promptly fleeced of his money by a confidence trick, he became innocently an agent for a crooked firm of "subscription publishers," and later a plain book agent. Then as tramp and hobo he explored a large section of the continent, winding up in the harvest fields of South Dakota, where certain injustices to floating labor caused him to go north, there to find what he sought in the soul of a people.

This is more than a narrative of adventure. It is a profoundly significant record of the attitude of the immigrant, more telling in its revelations of the inner mind and heart than of outward circumstances. After fifteen years' effort to find a publisher, this manuscript was withdrawn from circulation for a further period of seventeen years until the author reluctantly let friends take charge of it. This is unquestionably Canada's great book of the year.

William Arthur Deacon, *The Saturday Review of Literature* (London), May 5, 1928.

This search for America was not made in any such romantic fashion as that symbolized by the decorative Viking ship on the book's jacket. It followed, instead, the prosaic and rather painful way of open box-cars, of endless tramps alone or with dusty hobos, or perilous cindery journeys on the rods under passenger trains; and it ended with a handcar and a job painting signalposts. The America that is discovered is really only a segment of America: a vertical segment, composed of many layers, strata, of experience, and thrusting deep into the bed-rock of privation. But if it is only a segment, it touches an America that the average person does not know; cannot know. And it is a welcome antidote for the polite America of the European lecturer: the banquets, the flowers, the gently clapping hands. . . .

The story is not a treatise, but it often threatens to turn into a treatise. The Viking ship of adventure is forever becoming morassed in a Sargasso Sea of philosophical reflection. A certain amount of this is natural, inevitable. The newly arrived immigrant will pause to make comparisons, will take time to discard old erroneous theories and to adopt new erroneous theories; but the impression received is one of arrested movement.

The best part of the book is that which tells of what actually happens to Branden. The realistic method is splendidly suited to the swift-moving narrative, the marching sequence of exciting events. Especially remarkable for their qualities of biting reality are the accounts of the tramp to the west and the rod-riding episodes. In other parts of the book, the method is not so successful: the effort to expose every facet of thought and experience becomes faintly monotonous, and insignificant detail is wrapped in profundity. There is sincerity in the book, there is strength in it, there is deep and brooding intensity; but the imaginative power that would weld the enormous mass of material into a glowing whole is often lacking.

Manitoba Free Press, June 4, 1928 (unsigned). By permission of the *Winnipeg Free Press*.

Like most quest books worth the Baconian chewing, *A Search for America* raises more questions than the human mind will ever be able to answer this side of the millennium. It attempts nothing definite about America or about humanity, and its value is, of course, enhanced by its fairminded inconclusiveness. Mr. Grove is the civilized sort of author who suggests rather than asserts—indicates rather than concludes. In him you will come upon no take-it-or-leave-it rationale of all life; rather you will find chunks of raw experience and the day-by-day fluctuations of a person in search of himself. Ultimately Mr. Grove discovers what he wants to do with his own life; but he does not demand that the remainder of the earth's population follow immediate suit. . . .

A Search for America is one more bit of evidence that the older America of pre-immigration restriction meant all things to European men with careers to hew and livings to make. Mr. Grove first thought of it as a likely and easy spot in which to revive the family future. He chose it in preference to Australia or South Africa simply because the first steamer out of Liverpool was bound for Montreal. . . .

At times the narrative becomes chaotic. This is inherent in Mr. Grove's method, which is simply to take a phase or an incident and to write himself out. He says he has rewritten the book eight times—indicating trouble at condensation. Often his really important scenes receive less space than do the lesser happenings. With bows in the direction of our own taste, we would have been glad to have less about the mechanics and ethics of selling bad books and faked limited editions, and more of the days spent tramping and hoboing and working in the harvest fields of North Dakota. . . .

John Chamberlain, *New York Times Book Review Supplement,* December 30, 1928, 8. © 1928 by The New York Times Company. Reprinted by permission.

. . . An epic the power and color of whose telling only its readers can know. There are parts of it whose stark realism is unsurpassed in any book of its kind which we have read. And while certain criticisms, particularly those upon the difference between the theory and the practice of "equal opportunity" in the United States, may sting at times, reflection will prove them not unreasonable. That Mr. Grove could write as tolerantly as he does is our only wonder.

F. B., *Boston Evening Transcript,* January 23, 1929, 2.

Mr. Grove tells us that he wrote this interesting story thirty-two years ago and has rewritten it eight times. He calls it "the Odyssey of an immigrant." We do not know to what extent it embodies actual experience, but we should hardly think that the autobiographic hero, Philip Branden, was a typical immigrant. . . . It is soberly written, but not very convincing.

Saturday Review of Literature (London), August 31, 1929 (unsigned).

The Odyssey of an Immigrant is the sub-title of *A Search for America*. This book also is concerned with the rawness of America during a time within the memory of people not yet old, and it deserves commendation as the most distinctive thing of the kind published during recent years. The author is a Canadian. The adventures that are related occur mainly in the United States, and Mr. Grove is unusual in treating the two countries as members of a single civilisation. The book is written as the autobiography of a Scandinavian immigrant, partly Scotch in parentage and of exceptional culture. But it is obviously fiction, with a large basis of personal experience. Beginning his hero's adventures as a waiter in Toronto, Mr. Grove reveals the humours and scandals of bookselling by house-to-house canvass, and thereafter conducts his immigrant by river and road and by "beating it" on freight trains to the West. There are vivid descriptions of factory life and labour in the harvest fields, with an abundance of eccentric character and exciting incident. The book stands in a class of its own. It affords evidence of remarkable care in composition. The author says he has rewritten it eight times in thirty-two years. The statement is not hard to accept. But it is hard indeed to follow the ways of publishers in dealing with certain books from the other side of the Atlantic. *A Search for America* is an achievement by a Canadian writer of which the Dominion may one day be proud. It is sent out to the English public as printed in Massachusetts, and bearing the names of two American publishing firms.

New Statesman (*Autumn Books Supplement*), X (October 12, 1929), 34. By permission of *New Statesman*.

The fly-leaf of *A Search For America* describes it as epic, and grudgingly I allow that it is so. . . . It is a pity in a way that his observations were made too early to include the later developments in industry and advertising; but on the whole this is a gain, for, set beside the modern impressions, which are apt to read like a gossip-column, this book, which is splendidly oldfashioned, is a giant. Mr. Grove infuses magic into struggle and poverty, and gives more detail than a less able writer could successfully handle. He makes us thankful again for the fact that tramps seem to make such excellent philosophers.

Punch, or The London Charivari, February 26, 1930, 252 (unsigned).
© PUNCH, LONDON.

Other reviews of *A Search for America* noted: *The Whig-Standard* (Kingston, Ont.), November 26, 1927; *The Times Literary Supplement*, June 28, 1928; *New York Evening Post*, December 22, 1928; *Saturday Review of Literature*, March 16, 1929; *New York Herald Tribune*, May 12, 1929; *Sunday Times* (London), July 28, 1929.

Our Daily Bread (1928)

...*Our Daily Bread* is a story of the Canadian West during the past years of this century; it is a story of farming and drought, boom days and depression, but it is more than that. It is a true human drama—a drama of the realities of life as centred about the growth and development of the family of one John Elliot, a pioneer farmer of the short grass country of Saskatchewan.

"And his sons walked not in his way"—that in a word is the story of the book.

Here we have John Elliot—true son of the soil, looking forward towards the fulfilment of but one great desire—to found a family and to inroot himself and it into the soil —his soil, the soil he has worked and tilled and understands. But as his family grows, with slow and painful observation he sees something else happening. His children are his children, yet they are as diverse in their natures as the clouds in the sky, They, too, have desires and hopes, but they are different from his and so there follows the old, old story of filial and parental misunderstanding. John Elliot becomes what one of his sons-in-law all too understandingly calls "The Lear of the Prairies."

Our Daily Bread is simply told. There is no melodrama, no stirring conflicts. There is no need. The simple contrast and workings of human character need no elaboration. The reality is gripping enough and Mr. Grove has made it real. He has done it simply by taking each member of the Elliot family and showing how each different individual reacts to the environment of the family, and secondly, to the more important environment that each one has made for himself or herself through marriage and desire. . . .

As for the environment in which they lived and were raised, it will prove more than familiar to most of us! It is the prairies of the last decade and of this decade. The events of the boom days, and the war and the depressions, the big crops and the crop failures, the bonanza farming, and the economic problems, crop tenure, renting, bank loans, and the motor cars.

But above all this turmoil and stress of changing times stands John Elliot, dirt farmer, knowing his land, and his life work,—to make a home and a self-sufficient living. But his sons and his sons-in-law follow not in his ways. The transition to the age of machinery and finance is too much for them. The spirit of the age catches them and as crop failures come and go, high finance breaks down, and their free homesteads give way to crop tenury, "a state of things resembling feudal tenure."

But John Elliot can only look on and grieve, and philosophize over the actions of his children.

The inner essence of the book thus in time becomes the deep driving home of the old man's philosophy, or the philosophy of Frederick Philip Grove, as we believe he has embodied it in the utterances of John Elliot. It is the belief that the tilling of the soil, the creation of a living, and the raising of a family form the essential life. . . .

The reader may form his own opinions for or against
the age of machinery and finance, the transition period of
which caused such a chaos in the life of John Elliot. But
at least it must be admitted that Mr. Grove has woven a
living, vivid, withal a most homely and simple story about
that theme.

> "D.W.B.", *The Lethbridge Herald*, October 2, 1928. By permission of
> *The Lethbridge Herald*.

Mr. Grove's fifth published book, and third novel, is a
solid, distinguished piece of work, rather than an inviting
story. *A Search for America*, published last year and written
in 1894-95, was vital with the living yeast of a great faith
in the future of the Canadian West. *Our Daily Bread*,
written after the author had lived twenty years on the
prairie, is full of the discouragement of the settlers who
cannot make a go of it, who drag out their weary and
dispirited existences from one crop failure to another, and
of pessimism over the younger generation. It has none of
the tang of sharp drama of his *Settlers of the Marsh*. It is
drab but pure, framed to carry the burden of an old man's
disappointment as, bit by bit, approaching death renders
him more and more impotent. The whole conception is
grim, unrelenting, powerful and unlovely. . . .

> *The Mail and Empire*, Toronto, October 6, 1928 (unsigned). By per-
> mission of *The Globe and Mail*, Toronto.

If the name on the title page of *Our Daily Bread* were that
of a Scandinavian writer, the reader would feel no surprise
at the grim and unprepossessing reality which marks the
atmosphere of Mr. Grove's novel of the Saskatchewan
country. It is a sad tale of a man who loved the soil, who
wrested a comfortable existence from it, and who hoped
to see his children settled about him and following in his
footsteps. . . .

Our Daily Bread is probably one of the most depressing
tales penned by an American writer. There is no relieving
touch of humor or fancy, small departure in any case

from dull routine, sorrow and death. Mr. Grove, without question, has drawn a grim design and adhered closely to it. For all of that, the tale is curiously unrelated in its working out of character. The individuals are labelled, but there is no development which leads up to the result. Each and every one is tucked into a compartment and exhibited as mean, selfish, stupid, improvident or what you will—so long as it is disagreeable—without being given a chance for life. It is not possible to feel that Mr. Grove gave his poor people half a chance.

The New York Times, October 7, 1928, 20 (unsigned). © 1928 by The New York Times Company. Reprinted by permission.

It should be remembered first in regard to Frederick Philip Grove's latest book that it is only his second novel. He has achieved something like a personal repute through his character and history as recorded in part by two volumes of essays and an autobiographical narrative, *A Search for America*. This is an interesting thing. He is Grove and means something to intelligent Canadians regardless of the fact that he writes novels, as Dr. Johnson was and is Dr. Johnson regardless of *Rasselas*. And in my opinion this fact is likely to militate against his novels, causing them to be overpraised in some quarters, or depreciated by precisians.

This second novel should not convince any one that Grove is miscast as a novelist. He has a personal view of life though it is sometimes obscured, he has a sense of the ramifications of life, and he does not write badly. And this is an ambitious enterprise and it is not a failure. But neither is it notably successful, and it does not satisfy those expectations which his earlier work aroused.

It is to be seen that the faults of this book lie less in conception than in execution. Yet the writing itself is generally clear and unforced, save for a few natural inaccuracies like "an excessively small man" or "in fact when John did so without being asked, the old man grumbled;

and John, henceforth, left off doing so." And the movement of the story is lucid and consciously directed. There
is no deficiency in power of observation or in sincerity.
The next novel will be better; it may be what this one
might have been: great.

Raymond Knister, *Saturday Night*, October 13, 1928, 5. By permission
of *Saturday Night* and the Estate of Raymond Knister.

. . . During the first chapters we read with growing satisfaction. Here is the true farmer; a man of foresight,
thought, reflection; a man of influence, substance and
power. His name counts for all that is reliable and strong
in that section of the Canadian prairies where he has
developed his homestead, not for his family only, but for
future generations. To him farming is not merely an enterprise or a way of making money; it is the conscious and
continual act of creating that which is fundamentally
necessary and good—it is a way of life.

In boom periods he remembers the lean years; when
prices are down he works with the better seasons of yester-
day and tomorrow in mind. "Wheat's wheat," he says, "no
matter what it brings on the market." "Land has always
its value even though it may lose its price."

John Elliot's character is strongly conceived and the
diverse members of his ramified family are clearly defined,
but the portrayal is not so skilful as the conception is
strong. It lacks the subtle elements that make for style even
in the telling of a primitive tale.

And modern pessimism blights this story of achievement even as rust blights the wheatfields of the prairies. . . .

Caroline B. Sherman, *New York Herald Tribune*, October 14, 1928, 7.

Like its title this is a plain and substantial—and honest
—story of a large family in the Canadian Northwest. It is
interesting to note the cultural distinctions here exhibited
between the young frontier across the border and our own
older Main Street, to the advantage, on the whole, of the

former. There is not a touch of glamor—all homespun, which makes sober reading and thinking.

"R.H.," *The New Republic*, October 17, 1928, 256.

This second story by John Philip Grove [*sic*] is in its way quite as important a contribution to the fictional literature of Canada as is *A Search for America*, which after all cannot properly speaking be regarded as wholly a novel as it is more or less, rather more, biographical—a record of actual experiences told with an intensity of feeling that lifts it into a place entirely its own among books dealing with life and its spiritual and material development as viewed by the man, the young man, who comes to a New World to find its vaunted opportunities, material and spiritual. It is a great book, and I am not sure that *Our Daily Bread* is not also a great book, rugged and uneven though it may be at times. The difference between the two books—a thing that in no wise affects this later story—is the difference that lies between our inner and our outer selves; in the one Mr. Grove revealed the heart and soul and eagerness of the youth looking forward to life; in this present story he deals with results although the causes are not ignored. I wondered why he had not called his story "By Bread Alone" but perhaps that would have been too obvious; *Our Daily Bread*—so comprehensive is that word "our"—is not always bitter, hard though it may be to come by. . . .

While there are unevennesses in the writing, and while one may pause to wonder over certain conclusions and deductions, the fact that Mr. Grove has painted a notable picture in John Elliot and on a large canvas is certain. Some of the figures are blurred, nevertheless it is a work that cannot be ignored and that will not be forgotten. John Elliot stands out among Canadian creations, dominating and persistent and pathetic.

Margaret E. Lawrence, *The Evening Times-Globe*, Saint John, N.B., October 19, 1928. By permission of *The Evening Times-Globe*.

This is a Canadian story written by a Canadian and for some reasons it might be wished it were not. It is a sad and a depressing story, and one which cannot be said to breathe the spirit which permeates the people of this country. . . . There is no humour in it: there is none of the light and shade which are brought about by sunny, hopeful, cheery dispositions. It may be said that the whole outlook is dismal. Fortunately, as has been said, the story concerns a family of a generation ago—and the world changes.

The Whig-Standard, Kingston, Ont., October 20, 1928 (unsigned). By permission of *The Whig-Standard.*

Although he begins with the disadvantage of an over-worked background, a farm on the Canadian prairies, Mr. Grove has written an original novel. It is a study of John Elliot's patriarchal dreams and their failure and of his old age. The study of his old age is pre-eminently successful; it has a universal application which most highly localized novels lack. It traces with absolute sureness the death of Elliot's wife and his subsequent loneliness, his unhappy wandering from one to another of his nine children, the gradually increasing importance of phantoms in his life, and finally his faint but persistent delusions, in the pursuit of one of which he met his death. The story of his relationship with his children, although not as unusual as that of his decay into senility, is still good. The development of the character of each child is considered with reference to time and social condition as well as original temperament.

Our Daily Bread is pleasantly and faintly Victorian. Its plot progresses with logical smoothness; the greater part of the period that it covers is pre-war; and its vocabulary is straightforward and normal.

Boston Evening Transcript, October 27, 1928, 7 (unsigned).

Mr. Grove excels when he writes about himself, what he has gone through, what he has observed. His autobiographical writings have a sureness and depth, which makes him altogether notable, and *Over Prairie Trails* and *A Search for America* will not soon be forgotten. But when he overplays his personal record with invented scenes and characters and attempts a novel, the result is less impressive.

Our Daily Bread is enacted chiefly on the northern inhabited fringe of the prairie provinces. This is a country which Mr. Grove knows as well as any man, and the local colour of the tale is all that could be desired, save in quantity; we could wish for more. In the creation and reading of other people's characters—the prime requisite of good fiction—he is less convincing. We have only to compare the tale with *The Mayor of Casterbridge* which it obviously recalls, or with Mr. Grove's earlier personal narratives, to see the gulf between distinguished psychology and undistinguished. There is a world of difference between Mr. Grove setting his buggy desperately at a giant snowdrift or instinctively feeling his way to a vocation in the New World and these Isabels and Margarets, who are so hard to sort out as we read, and whose personal identity is lost when we shut the book.

Perhaps the fault—if we may use the word to indicate a certain disappointment—is one of technique rather than of creative power. Certainly, the story seems to call for a larger canvas than the author has given it. It tells of the slow break-up of John Elliot's family. His wife dies, the children marry and scatter, their ways are not his; at the end he is old and alone; with failing mind he tramps blindly to the old homestead to die there. This is clearly a tale in which the time-sense, the sense of things slowly changing, of people getting older, is all-important. We are frequently told of this, but we do not feel it all the time, as we do in *The Old Wives' Tale*, with its stealthy accumulation of detail and its persuasive suggestion of sands falling and clocks ticking. Mr. Grove has preferred the terser, more dramatic, more modern technique to the detriment of a theme which requires old-fashioned and leisurely treatment. If he had taken twice the space and indulged himself in the details of the pioneer life and landscape which he knows so well, his characters could perhaps have come to fuller life and he might have pulled off a great novel instead of just a good one.

Barker Fairley, *Canadian Forum*, October 1928, 66. By permission of Barker Fairley.

. . . The keynote of this book is power. There is power in the portraiture, power in the development of the story, power in the pictures of life on the land, and power in the handling of the various dramatic incidents that bring gloom and disillusion into John Elliot's later years. If those who can find time to try and belittle Mr. Grove's work possessed one-tenth of his power as a writer, they would probably discover better use for it than the futile waste of energy in decrying that which they are too pur-blind to understand. *Our Daily Bread* may not be a great novel. But it is without any doubt a powerful novel, a sincere novel, and the most encouraging sign that some-thing of the calibre of greatness may yet arise in Canadian fiction that I have read in twenty years. He deserves the thanks of all Canadians who have the courage to recognize that truth is not always honey and gingerbread. He has survived his early detractors, and he has shown the mettle of his spirit. I look for still stronger and more impressive work from his gifted pen.

S. Morgan-Powell, *The Montreal Daily Star*, November 3, 1928. By permission of *The Montreal Star*.

. . . The peculiar merit of the book seems to lie in its portrayal of John Elliot's character: the strength and clarity with which it follows his convictions, outlines the dominant qualities of his mind: his tenacious clinging to elementary Biblical standards in a world which is no longer elementary—or Biblical; his pathetic illusion, the age-old, egotistical illusion of the partiarch, concerning the continuance of personality in children. The portrait is not without a certain tragic power, but it does not seem to justify the immense significance piled up about it, the suggestion of greatness. And it is not great writing. It is nearer to court reporting.

Manitoba Free Press, November 5, 1928 (unsigned). By permission of the *Winnipeg Free Press*.

. . . There is much good descriptive writing in the book; it is vividly realistic, portraying with accuracy many of the vicissitudes of the frontier farmer. The picture of the mother is particularly well done; Mr. Grove knows the atmosphere of pioneering in its relation to the life of women. One wonders, however, whether he has not done the job too well. He intended to paint a drab picture but he has been so sparing with his bright colours that the dull shades almost lose their drabness. We cannot agree with the publisher's claim that the book presents "an honest picture of Canadian prairie life a generation ago." There may have been John Elliots but there were others —one could name many of them—who enjoyed the adventure of life and who asked much of it and were not disappointed.

"D.McA.," *Queen's Quarterly*, XXXVI (Winter, 1929), 181-183. By permission of *Queen's Quarterly*.

. . . A book is not necessarily high literature because it deals with "the land," though critical fashion inclines to the heresy. Mr. Grove's *Our Daily Bread* is a striking human document; but, since it cannot touch the spring of imaginative sympathy, since we close it with no sense of acquiescence, far less of enrichment, it does not rise into art. . . . It is infinitely depressing, this chronicle of mean and trivial children and a lonely old father. Certainly there is power in it; the phases of John Elliot's deathward journey, told with a simplicity that suits the matter, are harrowing enough. But there is no beauty of any kind, not even the beauty of completed pattern, to persuade the reader's assent.

Rachel Annand Taylor, *The Spectator*, CXLII (February 2, 1929), 169-170. By permission of *The Spectator*.

. . . Mr. Knister is intensive, Mr. Grove extensive, with a massive novel set in Saskatchewan, where the "nearby" little city of Kicking Horse is twenty-four miles from the farm and where "the whole landscape was suggestive of a sea with enormous billows gone rigid." It is a book of managed bigness, of many threads well held in hand, a book not timid to describe deaths by cancer and pneumonia, a book culminating in the senile journeyings and the death from exhaustion of John Elliot, "the Lear of the Prairies." "You can't fool the land," he cries, and, land-lover himself, he cared for his farm while money came almost by the way. It may, for all we know, be a just comment on the generation now middle-aged to say that they do not care for the land as their fathers did, but all John's family, from Cathleen, the smart townswoman to Henry, the lunatic, are failures in his eyes; nine are surviving at the end of the book, and such mass-production of disappointing offspring seems excessive. Opposed to them, certainly, the old Elliots may be conceded grandeur; individually, the children are ably characterised, and the career of each is traced with unflagging skill; collectively they are, if hardly degenerate, an improbably unfortunate lot, reducing by that weakness the book's noble ending to something a degree below tragedy.

H. B., the Manchester *Guardian*, February 8, 1929, 7. By permission of *The Guardian*.

. . . *White Narcissus* and *Our Daily Bread* are Canadian novels. One is soft-boiled and the other hard. The publishers are to be congratulated on starting a line in colonial fiction with "a country which has produced remarkably few novelists of a thoughtful variety." One is a wistful

little love story, mildly sophisticated, the other a typical
family epic in the American style. The idea is refreshing;
there must surely be many more colonies in which the
necessary condition, quoted above, will apply. Meanwhile,
Canada is behind Jamaica, which has quite a good novelist
within it, and a coloured expatriate outside.

. . . These books have finished this reviewer—more than
he could do for them—and tomorrow they will be left in
a hotel or dropped in the equable Adour, as he makes his
way still fleeing from simple people and those who write
about them, towards the snows of Aragon.

Cyril Connolly, "New Novels," *New Statesman*, XXXII (Feb. 23,
1929) 636-637. By permission of *New Statesman*.

. . . A sombre Canadian novel which leaves an impression
on the mind of strong and sober writing, and of life in Saskatchewan clearly depicted. . . . There is little that is
cheerful in this study, but Mr. Grove works on a big
canvas and has succeeded in differentiating his types and
making them real to us. He is not concerned with propa-
ganda, and indeed his Canadian family might belong to
any farming community, but the prairie landscape fills the
background and has become very vivid to us by the time
the tragic end of the book comes in sight. Tragedy walks
through it; the illness and death of Mrs. Elliot and the
consequent suffering of her husband and daughter are very
gloomy pages to read. John Elliot's passing seems merciful
by contrast. A writer of undoubted ability, Mr. Grove may
next time find a happier theme, or at least one that is not
so persistently melancholy as this deeply felt picture of
disaster.

The Times Literary Supplement, February 28, 1929. Reproduced from
The Times by permission.

The dust-cover of *Our Daily Bread* by Frederick Philip
Grove, using the words of a prominent critic (presumably
American) who read the manuscript, suggests that this "is

the first really *great* Canadian novel." It tells of a farmer whose far too numerous family break away from him and his dreams of a united community and effort. Mr. Grove will probably do something, but not this way. His multitude of characters, or rather names, bewilders; and so much happens—and most of it violent, or at least unpleasant—that it makes no impression. John Elliot "was a dreamer"; but "he had wooed and won that woman of women, his wife, with one single object in view: that of securing to himself the mother of his children. In the course of these many years twelve of them had arrived. Two had died; ten were living. Four great afflictions had visited him, ageing him before his time." . . . So our lavish author. But it will not do. Life is prolific; but, thank Heaven, not often as prolific as this.

> *The Observer*, Sunday, March 24, 1929, 9. By permission of *The Observer*.

Other reviews of *Our Daily Bread* noted: *Bookseller and Stationer*, October, 1928; *Calgary Daily Herald*, October 27, 1928; *Vancouver Province*, December 19, 1928.

It Needs To Be Said (1929)

The stalwart Manitoba novelist who has recently been lecturing in Eastern Canada here drops the mantle of storyteller and preaches a few sermons. He is a man of diverse talents. His first books to find publication were pleasant nature descriptions of prairie life. Then he took up the novel and tinged his chapters too often with what he calls "realism," but which went far into the sordid side of life. The present little book is a group of essays, or rather of supposed lectures to "a certain literary association." They comprise, doubtless, much of his literary creed, and in years to come they will have biographical interest.

There is a certain downright quality in Philip Grove,

and when he does not press his objectionable "realism" upon us he has an engaging directness and a descriptive power that have attracted many readers. . . .

M.O.H., *The Globe*, Toronto, March 30, 1929. By permission of *The Globe and Mail*, Toronto.

Frederick Philip Grove has given us another book and it will be a test for the reader to find how much gratitude he feels for the gift. It is a book about criticism and it contains much that has been said before in various forms and languages, but the title is fully justified—"It Needs To Be Said." The contents are really seven addresses and they are as direct and as unflinching as oral speech ought to be. If there are current banalities like "along these lines" and "reaction" we may excuse him on the ground of the necessity for being intelligible to his audiences. The book is a great book on the subject of criticism, and it is a real need in Canada. The thing we need most is public opinion, but there can be no public opinion worthy the name without a proper standard of criticism behind it. . . . Mr. Grove's book is a real addition to Canadian literature and should be read by all who make Canadian literature an element in their life and experience. . . .

The Hamilton Herald, April 5, 1929 (unsigned)

The tragedy of Mr. Grove's collection of sermons pointing the austere path of eternal glory in the arts is that most of those who will read them do not stand in need of his admonitions; and that those who need most the truths he delivers probably could not be induced to read his book. But Mr. Grove will not mind the tragedy; he has an essay here denouncing happy endings, and in other essays remarks more than once that a writer of genius must expect his reward from posterity. So, as to the whether "it" needed to be said, I am not sure; but I am glad it was said. This is an assertive little book, and therefore brave. From one standpoint or another, everything the author says about culture and literature and critical standards, and the rest of it, is true. But viewed from other angles, many of his assertions are debatable.

His primary aim is to divert the attention of Canadian writers from commercial success to high artistic achievement. Himself an artist, he can afford impatience with all printed matter that is not great literature: there is no room for anything but the highest. The critic cannot afford such impatience. If architecture decreed the poor man must destroy his house because not of perfect lines and the maximum of durability, the world would be homeless. "By that," the author retorts (p. 31) "he confesses he is no critic: for the only concern of the critic is with literary values."

But life is more than art, and the critic is no worse but better for knowing life beyond the confines of literature; and despite the danger of championing the second-rate, no one with any concern for cultural values, in the broadest sense, would wish the destruction of everything that did not measure up to Homer, Shakespeare, Dante and Goethe. Out of the bad comes the better, and out of the better the best. Pinnacles pierce the clouds only because their bases are set on the broad and common earth. A creed of masterpieces or nothing would lead precisely to—nothing.

Mr. Grove's excellent essay on "Nationhood" advocates Canada's continuation of the cultural tradition of Europe, as distinguished from the materialistic culture of the United States: and asserts that Canada's success in avoiding cultural and spiritual absorption in the United States is "an achievement of which we may justly be proud—more justly than of the extent and wealth of our country."

    The Mail and Empire, Toronto, April 13, 1929 (unsigned). By permission of *The Globe and Mail*, Toronto.

Although there is apparent diversity in them—"Realism in Literature," "The Aim of Art," "Literary Criticism," "Nationhood"—these seven lectures really converge at one point; they have one dominant purpose: to keep lit and

aflame the feeble guttering candle that is Canadian literature; to drive away the sinister influences that would snuff
out that candle; and to keep its essence clear and sure. . . .

There is a stringent, biting quality in some of Mr.
Grove's dicta—"the sweetish custard of our most successful
authors"—a vigorous soundness in many of his judgments;
but his writing sometimes gives an odd impression of in-
completed movement: of a mind in the grip of urgent and
compelling truths, but lacking somehow the power to
transmute that urgency and that compulsion to language.
Sometimes his truth flashes out, strong and clear and sure:
"Art . . . is of no nationality and of no time."—"Life . . .
must be reborn in the spirit"; sometimes it labors in the
meshes of pedestrian statement. In that sense the portent
of the book is often greater than its expression, the concept
greater than the performance. But these defects can be forgotten if the lectures serve to enliven in any way the feeble
guttering of the candle.

Manitoba Free Press, Winnipeg, July 1, 1929 (unsigned). By permission of the *Winnipeg Free Press*.

. . . The ordinary Canadian book-reviewer is not regarded
by Mr. Grove as a critic, and is thereby relieved of the
tremendous three-fold responsibility which rests upon that
priestly intermediary. He is perhaps permitted to say that
the essays are stimulating, sometimes because they are
provocative, as in "Nationhood," the least definite and
least judicial of the series, sometimes because they throw
light on the author's own attitude toward his art, as in
"Realism in Literature," sometimes because they are interesting bits of comparison under the guise of definition,
as in "The Novel." Many of us will disagree with much of
what Mr. Grove says: few will be found to dispute the
implication in the now somewhat overworked title. . . .

J. D. Robins *The Canadian Forum*, IX (August, 1929), 388-390.

Another review of *It Needs to be Said* appeared in *The
Gazette*, Montreal, June 1, 1929.

The Yoke of Life (1930)

. . . Mr. Grove has outdone himself, and in *The Yoke of Life* has written a great novel which, beyond any question, will stand the test of time. It is in striking contrast to *Our Daily Bread*, the comparatively loose and weak book he published last year. Its gloriously balanced form removes it from the class of *A Search for America*, whose autobiographical content prevented it from taking the shape of the perfect novel, which it did not really aim to be.

The Yoke of Life, in scene and tone, is more like *Settlers of the Marsh* than any of the other Grove books, but is a broader, deeper conception than *Settlers of the Marsh*, is written with greater effectiveness, and throbs with a concentration of passion and sorrow that Grove has nowhere else achieved. The inevitable comparison for *The Yoke of Life* is with Thomas Hardy's *Jude the Obscure*, the main theme being identical; and so it may be in order to say that Grove, when he wrote his novel, had never read a line of Hardy. Yet the parallels are so clear that many are sure to assume that *The Yoke of Life* is an imitation in a Canadian setting. . . .

. . . It is a strong end to a magnificent book. It suits my own taste that the novel should be so utterly authentic a description or dramatization of the place and period; but that is only an incidental. The crucial point is *The Yoke of Life* is a novel of power, plumbing the depths of an aspiring human soul, valiant unto death. Whether Len, at 20 or thereabouts, could have had sufficiently mature perception to foresee the future difficulties of life with Lydia, and to reach the decision he did at the Narrows, is beside the point. He is one of the very few characters in Canadian fiction who enslave the imagination of the reader; and the book is one that, I am sure, must be accorded classic rank immediately. A landmark has been set up.

For the benefit of younger writers I should like to mention that I have it on good authority that this novel has been repeatedly rewritten, in parts and in its entirety, several times since the first draft was completed. I read part of it in manuscript five years ago, or more, and it was complete in its original form several years before that. This critical care has contributed greatly, I believe, to the consummate craftsmanship which the book now exhibits. Everywhere the plot falls into a beautiful symmetry. The language is so plain as to conceal the art with which it is fitted smoothly together. No unnecessary word appears; and every scene furthers the action. From whatever standpoint one approaches *The Yoke of Life* and tests it, it proves itself a finished product, sturdy with an independent life of its very own. This is the way fiction ought to be written. Would that we had more stories so greatly conceived, and so faithfully executed to the smallest detail.

William Arthur Deacon, *The Ottawa Citizen*, October 11, 1930, 15. By permission of *The Ottawa Citizen*.

As in his preceding novel, *Our Daily Bread,* Mr. Grove is dismally preoccupied with the austere hardships of existence endured by Canadian backwoods settlers on government grant farms. . . .

. . . Though we are no advocate of forced happy endings, we found it somewhat of a trial, after following his misfortunes for 350 pages, to witness the death of Len, neither plausible nor inevitable, in a suicide pact with his sweetheart. Competently written, though rarely interesting, the story is one of the dreariest and most tedious we have read in many a day.

The Saturday Review of Literature, October 25, 1930, 274 (unsigned). By permission of *The Saturday Review*.

. . . During four-fifths of the story, until the end of the first chapter in Part Four, the book rests upon a realism which is expressed in masculine directness of style, which faces reality fearlessly, as Mr. Grove always faces it, but which also proclaims the fact of intelligent idealism with a forthrightness that should call for grateful appreciation. A courageous sanity characterizes this, the greater part of the book, both in manner and matter, and justifies the place of the author as the most thoughtful and competent writer of fiction in Canada today, or up to today.

But with the second chapter of the last part a change comes over it, and the inevitability is lost in the after-effects of fever. To be sure, the reader is prepared for the change, is prepared for the almost dream-like, symbolic quality in the concluding chapters, by the illness of the leading character, but he is not necessarily reconciled to it. Indeed, I am not sure after all that the reader has been sufficiently prepared for the terrible egomania into which the hero's outraged idealism is perverted. The introduction of a pathological explanation for action deprives the layman of all basis for criticism along the lines of consistency in character, but, though it silences, it does not always convince.

It may be that the real explanation lies in the obtuseness of the reviewer, but if this be true, the author has left his book open to the danger of misinterpretation by other readers of equal obtuseness. For such, the impression of a Hamsun's Glahn superimposed upon a Grove's Len Sterner results in an unhappy weakening of the final effect.

J. D. Robins, *The Canadian Forum*, February, 1931, 185-186.

. . . I give it as my considered opinion that *The Yoke of Life* is a great book, and I add that he whose critical capacity I most respect is of the same opinion. . . .

It was said once that the reason we get so few good books is that so few people who can write have anything to say, and that so few who have anything to say can write. Now it is obvious that the person who is going to write well of Canada must know much. A vast commerce with books will be indispensable, but even more indispensable will be a wide commerce with the world, and a profound, and hence imaginative, insight into life. I once heard Henri Bourassa laughing at the politicians and journalists who talk of a race question in Canada. "Why, we have fifty race questions in Canada, and it may not be fifty years before some of them will require to be answered." Not only is Mr. Grove's knowledge of European races, languages and histories exceptional; he has also studied their settlers in Canada as few other educated men have done. I have met missionaries to these north-west settlements, and journalists who had been among them all. But most missionaries and journalists in Canada are illiterate. Mr. Grove's knowledge of flora and fauna, geology and meteorology is just as striking. And, with it all, he has the observing eye of the poet. . . . The wilderness and its conquerors Mr. Grove takes as he finds them, loves them both, and so writes as man writes best—out of a great sympathy and love.

Carleton Stanley, *Dalhousie Review*, XI (January, 1931), 554-561. By permission of *Dalhousie Review*.

Stories of pioneer life and lumber camps will always have their interest, for they stir the imagination with their powerful struggle against strong external forces and they introduce the town dweller to a world of sheer action. This always excites, but Mr. Grove's latest novel, *The Yoke of Life*, fails of that effect. The author's knowledge of his setting gives the impression of having been culled from books, and even then he has used this material only as a background for his own reflections on life. These would not have been so ineffective had they been used simply and as the natural outcome of the story, but Mr. Grove insists upon being literary at all costs, and even at lumber camps men talk only as they do in nineteenth-century melodramas and they think in words which philologists would envy. . . .

It is a great pity that Mr. Grove did not submit himself to a simpler rendering of this excellent material.

A review of *The Yoke of Life* also appeared in the New York *Herald Tribune,* December 7, 1930.

Fruits of the Earth (1933)

. . . What the pioneers have done makes a thrilling story, however, and this novel tells how Manitoba was settled in the years just before and just after the War. It is a novel of Empire in the best sense, a contribution to history as well as an entertaining tale. . . .

There are not many novels of Canadian life, and few that are notable; but this is certainly a great book.

Robert Gernon, *Everyman,* February 4, 1933.

The author of *Search for America* and *Our Daily Bread* here gives us a vivid picture in our West. . . .

We have here an ambitious story, indeed, but one told with sympathy and understanding. . . .

The book is worth while as a careful and intelligent study of human nature, human aspiration and human failure.

W. R. R. in *The Globe,* Toronto, February 18, 1933. By permission of *The Globe and Mail,* Toronto.

This is a story of a farm in Manitoba which makes its very considerable effect by sheer weight of detail, truthfully, relentlessly accumulated.

. . . This brief account cannot explain the unsentimental interest of the book. Mr. Grove succeeds in making us feel something of the nostalgic call of the prairie which absorbs the spirit of man into itself. Without partisanship, or heat, he also voices the farmer's wife whose life is one long monotony of work, who grows shy and savage for want of human contacts, whose husband is faithful to her simply because his whole energy and emotion go to the earth.

The Times Literary Supplement, February 23, 1933, 128 (unsigned). Reproduced from The Times by permission.

In saying that Frederick Philip Grove's new novel, *Fruits of the Earth*, is far below his own standard, as set in *Settlers of the Marsh* and *The Yoke of Life*, I do not mean that it is worthless, nor must specific objections that follow be so read. Once Mencken spoke of the heavy-footed Dreiser plodding his lonely way across the otherwise blank page of American literature. This is not quite true; but, so far as it is true something similar could be said of Grove and the Canadian novel during the past ten years. Everything he writes has a certain seriousness and maturity and distinction, making it well worthy of consideration now. He is due to be the first Canadian novelist to have his work survive him in a complete or definitive edition.

. . . While the author's aim has been confused, his attention spread rather meaninglessly over a number of things, (and the book therefore fails as a novel) Grove has painted a memorable picture of a Manitoba pioneer community for such as desire to be informed about that sort of life. One cannot forget the drainage ditches and their importance to crops. The writing, for the most part, is good, as we should have expected it to be. . . .

William Arthur Deacon, Montreal Daily Herald, February 25, 1933.

. . . The narrative deals with every phase of that prairie life, the seasons in their order year by year, and the crops, the school, local politics, and human nature generally. The proverbial acquiring of the latest machinery, the building of barns and a large house, and all the equipment belonging to a great farm enter into the narrative. It is a farmer's tale, and Mr. Grove is an author who knows how the soil grips the heart of a man. And his narrative is vivid. He has either worked on a farm, or else kept his eyes wide open while going here and there in the country. A poignant part of the story is the death through accident of Spalding's beloved little boy.

The Bookman, *Winnipeg Free Press*, February 25, 1933. By permission of the *Winnipeg Free Press*.

. . . This is no flippant novel dashed off at random, but a deep life study, a full-length portrait of a man from youth to old age, struggling with nature in the raw. From the standpoint of success in farming it is a stirring story, notably the details of how Abe Spalding harvested and saved the mighty crop from his two square miles of land in 1912. Coast readers will find here a cross-section of life on the prairies, including the struggle of the foreign immigrants, that will prove a revelation. It is written with infinite patience and is stamped with the hallmark of a sincere, far-seeing writer. . . .

E. H. Scott, *The Province* (Vancouver), February 26, 1933. By permission of *The Province*.

. . . The book is far, far more than a tale of pioneer work in Manitoba. It is a piece of history, an invaluable and authentic picture of the real life on the prairie farm, and as such it must take its place with the comparatively few authentic novels of our decade.

Power is one of the central themes, and power reverberates throughout the book. The power of the whole story is outstanding. It impresses you more and more as you read. It is the power of a writer who knows what he wants to say, how to say it, how to draw portraits that live on the printed page, how to describe life in terms of flesh and blood, not in terms of a text book or a philosophy. There is drama here—the stark, vital drama of man's struggle with, and conquest of, the soil; and if at times the vision seems overwrought with gloom and there are ruthless passages, it must be borne in mind that Grove is resolute to tell the whole truth as he has known it and not to gloss over anything and thus strike a false note. He is never coarse, and he is never brutal. He writes as a man who has fought a bitter fight with life in the raw, and who, though he has won, has not come through the battle unscathed, but still retains his high courage and his faith in humanity.

It is pleasant to contrast such work as this with some of the trumpery stuff that has been handed to us with the assurance that here is the realistic Canadian novel. The work of Frederick Grove puts such meretricious insincerities to shame. Here is a man who can write of Canada in a way that should make Canadians proud. He has done a fine work in this book, and it is assured of a permanent place in Canadian fiction. We have need of such writers here and of such strong, impressive and gripping tales.

S. Morgan-Powell, *The Montreal Daily Star*, March 11, 1933. By permission of *The Montreal Star*.

. . . The novel is in the Hardy tradition and philosophy. Fate is neither kind nor cruel, but inexorable and she has habitation within and without those she harries. The prairies, great and grey and uncommunicating, are the background of the story and in one noteworthy chapter they become a character in the novel as Egdon Heath became a character in *The Return of the Native*.

Mr. Grove has represented the prairies truthfully. It is questionable whether he has *interpreted* them truthfully. To the prairie-born they can mean, not only the late grey rains of autumn in the quickly shortening days, dawns and dusks and the eternal half-lights of the dead land, but also the rich afternoon sun of late summer when the wheat is a yellow sea, and the full harvest moon when it stands in the stooks, and above all the warm, searching spring winds that stir the earth to open to new seeding and to send life again into the long green and brown grasses that wave over her.

Mary Davidson, *The Twentieth Century*, March 15, 1933. By permission of Twentieth Century Magazine, Limited.

. . . I consider this novel to be exceedingly impressive, well-written, and vivid, and at times really exciting. I must add—this is not a quotable adjective—that I also find it slightly irritating. . . .

. . . His book is something more than an accurate record of the growth of a district; it is a document of modern Canada.

John C. Moore, *The Bookmark*, Spring, 1933, 20-21. Reprinted by permission, THE BOOKMARK.

Frederick Philip Grove's novels seem to go in pairs. *The Yoke of Life* was matched with *Settlers of the Marsh*, and now *Fruits of the Earth* is matched with *Our Daily Bread*. Abe Spalding of the new novel is a better John Elliot. He extends his ambition and his influence from the family to the community; he is a bigger man, but the problem of *Fruits of the Earth* is fundamentally the same as the problem of *Our Daily Bread*; the individual standing out against changing society.

In many respects, *Fruits of the Earth* is better than its predecessor. It is tighter, although it does lose its grip and go spluttering at the end; it has perhaps a wider significance; yet Grove's old faults, prudery and pedantry, dog it down.

Dog it down, one might go so far as to say, to the point of preventing it from being a novel. "Partly because he reverenced facts and had no faculty it seems (his language is meagre and unmetaphorical) for impressions, it is doubtful whether his choice of a novelist's career was a happy one." These words, spoken by Virginia Woolf of a writer in a vastly different world, might have been said of Grove.

The book lacks that human warmth without which no novel can live—is it significant that Grove has more success describing a snowstorm than a sultry summer day? Thus far, he always says, but no farther. The picture of Abe, the homesteader, working until dark, driving his plowshare into the unbroken prairie, is almost thrilling. We almost become conscious of Man and the Prairie making a pattern together in the cosmos, but the writer grimly forbids; he downs our emotion, our soaring imagination, with his precise dead words: "He had the peculiar feeling as though he were ploughing over an appreciable fraction of the curvature of the globe." Whenever Grove looks up out of his facts and makes a concession to humanity, it is with a gesture self-conscious and unconvincing. The little lad Charlie is just such an awkward, half-formed gesture, as if Grove, like Abe, was afraid to trust himself.

Abe Spalding, ambitious, proud, honest, shrewd, who humbled the prairie, fought its floods and droughts and bullied it into yielding, and who was struck down by his very victory, might have been a figure of tragedy. But his stern, upright sense of duty betrays itself, after all, as harsh vanity. He blames himself for the new times that creep into the district: he should have been stronger, he should have stemmed them. When he marches into the schoolhouse and puts an end to the dance, like a prophet from the Old Testament, after telling his wife "I shall have to take office again," he becomes a figure ridiculous in his pious ego. Had Grove realized this, he might have made him pitiable, the giant trying to stem the tide of the world —perhaps there is always a little of the ridiculous in the heroic—but Grove apparently did not see the irony.

Unsatisfying as a novel, *Fruits of the Earth* is nevertheless a valuable book, and its value lies entirely in the writer's passion for facts. *Fruits of the Earth* is important as a social document. Where else have we such a complete, detailed picture of the building up of a new community on the Canadian prairies? The drama of this book is the drama of facts, or events. It is the drama of petty politics, ditches, roads, labour problems, the price of flax, farming methods. These are real things, significant steps in the history of Canada, and we welcome a writer with keen observation who sets them down with energy and accuracy. As Grove presents them, the fight to save the crop from flood, the boom in flax, the building of a school, are far more absorbing than the fall from virtue of Abe's young daughter. Had the historian been courageous and single-minded enough to reduce his human figures to their proper perspective, *Fruits of the Earth* would have been a better book.

Robert Ayre, *The Canadian Forum*, April, 1933, 271. By permission of Robert Ayre.

. . . *Fruits of the Earth* is a book of noble quality, grandly planned and admirably executed. I have no idea how well it will sell: had it been published ten years ago it would have been a best-seller, but today, when other styles are in fashion, it may not gain the success it deserves. But at least I can do my best to recommend it.

. . . Its outstanding merit lies in the picture of Abe Spalding and in the background of his harsh farming experiences. I presume that Mr. Grove is a Canadian; if he is, this is the first book from that country that I have read in recent years which achieves greatness. Perhaps I over-estimate its merits, but I have put it on my shelves beside *Main Street* as a pioneer work of real significance.

C. E. Bechhofer Roberts, *New English Weekly*, London, June 15, 1933.

Two Generations (1939)

A new novel from Frederick Philip Grove, author of *A Search for America*, and recipient of the Gold Medal of the Royal Society of Canada in recognition of his services to Canadian literature, is a literary event. *Two Genera-tions* tells, with power and sincerity, of life on a farm in south-western Ontario, north of Lake Erie. The theme is wider than that, however, being nothing less than the theme of a Lear forced to divide up his kingdom, the theme of the three strong sons of a masterful father, grow-ing up to seize their place in a world still dominated by the father, the theme of the conflict of two generations, with right on both sides. The book should satisfy two different sorts of talkers about "Canadian" literature. It should satisfy those who claim, somewhat narrowly, that all truly Canadian literature must have a typically Cana-dian setting and characters, for if a setting confined to two farms in Norfolk county, with references to Toronto and Kitchener and Hamilton is not Canadian, what is? It should satisfy those, too, who believe that setting is a minor and accidental note in a work of art, that a great novel is more than a matter of place-names: it is a matter of uni-versality of theme.

This universal theme is well worked out in Mr. Grove's new novel. The father is magnificently drawn, and so too is the mother. The three sons are clearly differentiated, al-though perhaps only the youngest, Philip, is as fully developed as one would like. The daughter is sympa-thetically handled, and the remaining characters adequately sketched in, with the exception of Nancy, the dancer who marries George. One feels that she requires an exotic flight beyond Mr. Grove's range. I particularly liked the glimpses of Henry's Cathleen and the fashionable aunt. The characters are engaged in a definite struggle for indepen-dence, or domination, or subsistence, or education, and the clash of character and aim provides the story, which is sufficiently gripping to hold the reader without the aid of melodrama. I was afraid that the Christmas snowstorm was going to be employed as a "Deus ex machina," but Mr. Grove kept the proceedings on the normal level, and worked out his conclusion quietly and authoritatively in terms of character.

This is a substantial and meritorious novel, the fine qualities of which outweigh its defects. Mr. Grove has never been a slick writer. I imagine he is a most painstaking one, with a schoolmaster at one elbow, and an evangelist at the other. Perhaps that is why much of his dialogue reads as if it were a poor translation. His descriptive writing, too, is more conscientous than imaginative; sometimes rather a catalogue than a picture. However, these are minor criticisms. The spirit of this novel is right, and it tells a moving and holding story with power and insight and sincerity. I wish we had more Canadian novels on the same level.

W. S. Milne, *Saturday Night,* August 5, 1939, 9. By permission of *Saturday Night*.

. . . Mr. Grove has given us, in *Two Generations*, his best book; and that means one of the best novels ever written in Canada. This story of the joint and several rebellion of a prosperous farmer's children of the average age of 21 is true to four separate sets of principles. It is true to the deep facts of human nature in general; that is a fundamental. It is also beautifully and meticulously true to environment. Normal rural life in Southern Ontario is adequately portrayed, with all little touches of a writer who has seen himself twelve years a farm labourer and is now a farmer in the district of which he writes. For the sake of general reception, it is a happy circumstance that Mr. Grove has not only remembered the novelist's prime duty of delivering a story, but that it is an easily grasped story, a story that will be thoroughly enjoyed apart from every other merit.

Two Generations is fourthly, true to art—a matter that will not affect its immediate popularity much, but will probably prolong its existence. Its chief literary merit is a rigorous simplicity. Nothing happens but what advances the action; the diction is direct, never fancy. The impression is that everything needful to complete understanding is told, and the narrative is never encumbered with the needless. There are some striking passages. The description of the Christmas storm, for instance, recalls Mr. Grove's two volumes of splendid essays about Manitoba landscape and weather; yet these do not appear as embellishments, but only as backgrounds essential to action. . . .

W. A. Deacon, *The Globe and Mail*, Toronto, August 5, 1939. By permission of *The Globe and Mail*, Toronto.

When reviewers say, as many have said, that this is Frederick Philip Grove's best novel, do they mean that this is his best book outright or do they distinguish between his novels proper and his more personal volumes? My feeling about him all along has been that he is strongest where he is most autobiographical and that his personal record in *A Search for America* and *Over Prairie Trails* has a force, an intensity which has little to gain from any admixture of fiction. His novels, again, always seemed best to me in those episodes and characters that were nearest to his own struggles and to his own temperament. As with many other novelists, though not with all, autobiography appeared to be the right approach to an understanding and judging of his work.

Two Generations compels one to re-consider this opinion. Its sub-title describes it as "a story of present-day Ontario" and we know that Grove has only comparatively recently lived in that part of Canada, his middle years having been chiefly spent in the West. Clearly then the story comes out of his foreground rather than his background. And there is everything in the narrative itself to show that while drawing, as it must, on the author's experience and especially on his farmer's knowledge, it does not reach very deep into his personal life, as do the two books above-mentioned, but is primarily a novel in the stricter sense that it deals with invented characters and situations not rooted in the private life of the author. At least I would hazard the statement that *Two Generations* is less autobiography and more novel than any of Grove's previous books.

It is a study of family life in one of the more settled and prosperous parts of rural Ontario. There is an echo of pioneering days in the character of Ralph Patterson, the father, but even he goes into the city dairy business, though not with profit to himself. Of his children one marries a professional dancer and gets involved in the naughty world; another urbanises himself to the extent of turning florist and painting his delivery vans mauve with yellow lettering; two others put themselves through a higher education in Toronto and bring modern philosophy back with them to the farm. All of which is stubbornly resisted by the unprogressive and tyrannical but not wholly unattractive father, whose spiritual defeat it is the tale's chief business to record. One by one his grown-up children shake off his invisible grip and act for themselves —the mother always understanding, the father never. The issue is sharpest with the third son, Phil, after which there comes a reconciliation and a change of heart. But whether Tom and Mary, who have yet to break away, go through the same crisis is left uncertain. The book makes each of its characters so clearly separate and alive that one can't help wondering what these two younger ones are like. Anyway, I am suspicious of "changes of heart."

Here then, as I have tried to indicate, is a really authentic short novel about the Ontario we know—it dates strictly speaking in the late nineteen twenties—epitomizing the semi-urban, semi-rural life which give the last ten or twenty years in this province their peculiar transitional character. How many households, reading these pages, will be compelled to exclaim—not necessarily at every point, but certainly at many—"This is us, exactly." The pressure of this thought will ensure that the book will go from hand to hand and be widely read—more widely, I suspect, than any of Grove's earlier books. If young Canadians read it, it will do something towards correcting their sense of literature where it most needs correcting. I refer to that devastating sense of literature as something divorced from life—the "literary" sense of literature—which has done and is still doing much harm in our schools. Perhaps there is no Canadian book that could do more to obliterate that fatal notion. The best thing about *Two Generations* is precisely this—that it is not literary at all in the horrible Ontario sense of the word, but that it is, both in style and in conception, the real, the honest thing, unfalsified and even ungraced.

One more point. If we compare this book with any earlier book by the same author we notice a change. For one thing, it is lighter in handling than the earlier Grove books, further from the tragic and nearer to high comedy in the good old sense of the word. It has a greater speed and vivacity of action and dialogue. It is in every way a more modern book than its predecessors. This is peculiarly gratifying, because Grove is now in his upper sixties and can only have written this book in quite recent years. Remembering, as we must—however regretfully—that the history of Canadian literature—and of Canadian painting too—is full of names of those who never did anything new after the age of forty, we may conclude by paying Grove the compliment of saying that in his latest book he has shown his juniors in the country that he is younger than most of them and that premature senility is not a necessary condition for authorship.

Barker Fairley, *Canadian Forum*, October, 1939, 225. By permission of Barker Fairley.

. . . A powerful study, written out of full knowledge, and yet with great imaginative sympathy, of the social and economic change affecting "life on the land" in Canada. The characters of this novel are deeply etched, and unforgettable. Mr. Grove has here done for southwestern Ontario what his other books have done for the prairies—caught Canadian life, and caught it in 'accents of the eternal tongue.'

Carleton Stanley, *Dalhousie Review*, XIX, (1930-1940), 129-130. By permission of *Dalhousie Review*.

Two Generations is a work in the classic tradition, restrained, balanced and economical of words. . . . The scene of *Two Generations* is western Ontario, and all the references (for there are no long descriptions digressing from the main theme) show keen personal observation and deep attachment to that land. The people are people of today, the solid and intelligent farming community of a region which is settled, but not yet so removed in time from pioneer conditions that all the repercussions of that earlier life have died down. The conflict between the dominating father, who is the main character of the book, and his sons, developing under changed social conditions, with the well-balanced mother as a mediator, is profoundly interesting and well understood. Ralph Patterson's autocratic character, able and strong as he is, leads his family into an extremely complicated situation; and the author has transformed this occasion of conflict, Canadian as it is in every actual detail, into something universal in its quality. Tragedy there is, but a power of acceptance goes with it. The book leaves one with a feeling of satisfaction, in its completeness, sincerity, and power of impact; and in addition to all considerations of technical method or of philosophical conceptions of human nature, it is a keenly interesting story.

"E. H. W.," *Queen's Quarterly*, XLVI, (Autumn 1939), 380-381. By permission of *Queen's Quarterly*.

. . . The main design of character and situation is well developed. Especially memorable is the fierce and subtle conflict of temperament between Phil and his father, and the sympathetic characterization of Mrs. Patterson, the wisest person in the novel, with her affectionate understanding for both generations, and her ability to control both in a quiet fashion. Unfortunately the peripheral characters and themes are much less satisfactory. One gets the impression that Mr. Grove may in his innocence have added them to make the book "popular." One son marries a professional dancer, who brings a French maid and nightclub atmosphere back to the old farm, and of course there is the anticipated adultery and divorce. Another daughter-in-law is made feminine to a pathological degree, and there is some curious semi-Freudian analysis of Ralph Patterson's dark moodiness. Almost as surprising in a book by Mr. Grove is the easy success achieved by some of his characters. They plant hundreds of acres in the spring, and after the pleasant interlude of summer, they bank thousands of dollars in the fall. They surprise even the suave salesmen with their lavish ways when buying automobiles and electric milkers. Phil and Alice find it delightfully easy to cultivate a farm and to come first and second in the province at the examinations for university matriculation. In spite of the fine things in *Two Generations* one feels that the author has for once gone off on a false trail. He has often stated that the north, and the hardships of the worker on the soil, are his proper subjects. Southern Ontario fails to incite his full descriptive power in this novel, and there is not much authentic hardship. Even Ralph Patterson longed for a more strenuous kind of existence.

J. R. MacGillivray, *University of Toronto Quarterly*, IX (April 1940), 292. By permission of University of Toronto Press.

The Master of the Mill (1944)

. . . The theme of the tale is that modern industry and finance are not only destroying democracy but breaking the back of humanity. As new machines destroy handwork most men and women will be forced on the dole, save for the human robots tending the machines and the crooks who think they are in command when in reality they are slaves of a system.

Of course any author has the right to his opinions, however distorted and unreal. If he prefers to distribute them in a work of fiction that also is his right. But one would expect him to be an adept in that artistic field, to make his characters continually credible and to tell his story directly rather than indirectly.

This novel is built of the cloudy recollections and thoughts of a man in senility, of the confidences between the rich daughter-in-law and upper servant (highly improbable) and in bits of a prospective history written by the General Manager of the mill. But all these people talk like the author rather than like themselves.

So, to one reader, the atmosphere of unreality hangs over even the realistic passages of description and dialogue. For Mr. Grove writes well. He would write better if he were not trying at the same time to do something he considers more important.

> J. E. Middleton, *Saturday Night*, January 20, 1945, 19. By permission of *Saturday Night*.

At the age of 73, Frederick Philip Grove has given us his most thoughtful and technically most complicated work. His appearance, 20 years ago, brought a new seriousness to the Canadian novel; and the fact that *The Master of the Mill* has been 14 years under construction is typical of his deliberate, careful craftsmanship. Though perhaps no longer than *A Search for America*, which is his most popular book, *The Master of the Mill* consumes more time in the reading because the earlier story was the adventure tale of an immigrant, while his latest is a dramatization of his mature views of what the machine will do to human society in the near future.

. . . The new novel reads like a valedictory and its

breadth of sympathy with all his many characters indicates a welcome mellowness of outlook.

It is not character, however, that is the governing impulse of this novel, though some experts believe it always should be, and even though *The Master of the Mill* contains a magnificent portrait gallery, in which we recognize J. S. Woodsworth and other people we have known.

Behind the three generations of Clarks, who owned, in turn, the colossal flour mill in the vicinity of the Lake of the Woods, there is the problem of the extent to which the mill was created by Rudyard Clark, the old miller, who perpetrated one crime that the mill might grow, the extent to which his son Samuel, the designer, was responsible for the direction of that growth, and the degree of blame or praise properly belonging to the grandson Edmund, who saw in the flour mill only an instrument of economic power.

Clever and tricky in delivery, *The Master of the Mill* is a fascinating specimen of shifting focus. That is what will make it difficult for many to read, and that is also the secret of a strength and balanced artfulness which rates the book among the half-dozen best Canadian novels ever written.

Make no mistake about the basic theme. It is the effect of this gigantic, wholly automatic mill on the lives of owners, workers, management and the community at large even beyond our time. To make that into a story, a convincing narrative of human interest, Mr. Grove has had not only to go into the personal lives of the three Clark men, but also of the wives and other associates. It is a remarkable feat to have wormed so deeply into the contrary motives of types so widely different in nature. That can be done easily if a story is long enough.

What makes Mr. Grove's technique dangerously complicated is lack of unity in the viewpoint of the narrators. For the central character is Senator Sam Clark in his extreme old age. The dramatic incidents in the history of the mill are evoked erratically in the memory of the man, who has already half withdrawn from life. Some of these scenes and persons are known to us through the eyes and in the words of Lady Clark, Sam's daughter-in-law; others we hear about from Miss Charlebois. One chapter is from the pen of Captain Stevens, a mill executive. A good deal of the time we are among the kaleidoscopic recollections of the Senator. More rarely, the author intervenes with information or helpful comments.

All these necessary parts, without any more obvious chronology than the vagaries of a senile memory, are put together in a sequence that ultimately works into a rich pattern; but the long periods of suspense, waiting for the parts to fuse into comprehensive coherence, may weary the impatient reader. Those who have patience will be rewarded by an illuminating implied commentary on our industrial civilization. They will see bankers, lawyers, engineers, mill hands and politicians playing out the great drama of power in terms of our own age and country, and even in the figures of a score of famous Canadians, more or less altered to fit their functions in the story. At this level of skill we have not seen anything like this before.

In saying that *The Master of the Mill* is a brilliant novel of social significance, showing masterly architectural virtues in construction, I do not mean that there are no flaws. The concentration demanded of the reader is a handicap; not everybody will wish to work so hard in his hours of recreation. An occasional sentence might be reworded in the interests of clarity, even to avoid ambiguity, though the writing as a whole is extremely careful.

. . . Flaws are trivial, merits substantial. A more straight-away recital would have lacked in subtlety. There would have been technical difficulties in bridging time-gaps. As it is, *The Master of the Mill* is an adroit patchwork of exquisite bits of self-revelation. Each poignant passage is vivid within its own circumference. Whatever is found disconcerting in the sudden transitions between present, past and future was a necessary device to keep the story within 400 pages and at equal emotional tensions, though a mind already confusing the identities of wife, sweetheart and daughter-in-law, is not the best window through which to attain absolute coherence of vision.

The ambitions of the Clarks, the strikes of the men, above all, the beautiful structure and mechanical perfection of the mill itself, have been combined in a splendid, noteworthy novel that is ideal for the thoughtful reader.

W. A. Deacon, *The Globe and Mail*, February 10, 1945, 8. By permission of the *Globe and Mail*, Toronto.

. . . In this latest book, *The Master of the Mill*, upon which Mr. Grove says he has been working many years, the ugliness, the negation of humanity, and the powerlessness of mankind to keep control of the machine and economic forces which itself has invented, are most powerfully described. . . .

I found *The Master of the Mill* difficult reading. At first I attributed the difficulty to my own conservatism, and dislike of the "flashback" method of the "movies." I did not guess, all at once, that the book had been laboured over for long years, touched up here, and touched down there, until important and character-making episodes were dealt with by a mere innuendo. It is not a novelty, on the part of dramatists or novelists, to ask us to trace a development through three generations of a family. But it is something of a novelty to make us see these three generations through the dazed and nearly insane mind of a man of eighty-three, who has long outlived the third generation as well as the first. This man is greatly influenced by three women who all bear the name of Maud—one his secretary, one his wife, one his daughter-in-law. At the end, in his mind, the two latter Mauds are extremely confused: he thinks he is talking to one when he is really talking to the other. The footman closes the door of the limousine, driven swiftly by a capable chauffeur, but immediately we realize that we are in an open horse-drawn vehicle, driven by the character himself, at a period exactly forty years earlier. One realized long ago that Mr. Grove was extremely well-read in the French novelists, but has any French novelist been as subtle as Mr. Grove? . . .

But when will North Americans catch up with Philip Grove? In particular, will an adequate number of Canadians be shaken out of complacency by Mr. Grove's grave warning, or by any other means, in time to avert a measureless disintegration?

Carleton Stanley, *Dalhousie Review*, XVX, (1945), 173-181. By permission of *Dalhousie Review*.

. . . *The Master of the Mill* by F. P. Grove is likewise unusual in construction and pretty forbidding to the irresolute. Old Senator Clark, living in princely luxury, surrounded by a retinue of devoted retainers, looks out across his domain to the flour-mill which has been the source of his wealth, a wonderful structure that resembles an Egyptian pyramid from without and is the Factory of the Future over the Grand Central Terminal within. Then he begins to relive his whole life in memory, with incredible circumstantiality calling up conversations, scenes, or feelings, and helped from time to time by his feminine companions who have the same powers of detailed recollection. He becomes a trifle confused, however, in some of his memories (and the reader will sympathize), for the three women who were to have the largest influence on his life were by some baptismal oversight each named Maud. The mood is one of regret. The senator has tried to be a fine man and share the wealth; indeed he is almost a socialist in some of his views; but the domination of his less altruistic father and son, the appalling efficiency of the mill, and the shocking way wealth has of begetting wealth, made him a multi-millionaire in spite of all he could do. Among the strange scenes which linger in the memory one might mention those in the huge glass-walled gymnasium where the senator's lady and her friends take their exercise on the flying-trapeze, and any of those involving that wonderful old-time vamp, Sibyl, for example, when after a ball she drives down the street in an open landau with six men toasting her in champagne. The literary editor of a Toronto newspaper gives his considered judgment that this book is "among the half-dozen best Canadian novels ever written," and the spokesman for Mr. Grove's publisher asserts on the dust-cover that it is "unquestionably his masterpiece." One naturally hesitates to dissent when persons who have read widely can be so sure, but it seems to me that the first holds far too low an opinion of Canadian fiction and the second is unjust to all of Mr. Grove's earlier, and often excellent, writing.

J. R. MacGillivray, *Letters in Canada: 1944*, *University of Toronto Quarterly*, XIV, (April, 1945), 271. By permission of University of Toronto Press.

. . . The narrative is endowed with a pity and a wisdom that are more eloquent than the theorizing. There are also not a few dramatic episodes, but the constant effort to synthesize fiction with thesis and exposition and the frequent shiftings of the point of view somewhat impair the validity of the story as a work of art. Yet it repays the reading, and the appearance of several well-known Canadian figures under fictitious names enlivens two of the later chapters.

G. H. Clarke, *Queen's Quarterly*, LII, (Summer, 1945), 254-5. By permission of *Queen's Quarterly*.

In Search of Myself (1946)

Twenty-one years ago a novel was published in Canada which caused more than a little sensation. Its title was *Settlers of the Marsh*, and it was written by Frederick Philip Grove, then a professor in a western university. It told, vividly and realistically, of conditions among a certain section of foreign settlers in the Canadian West.

It is a matter of genuine satisfaction to me that I was among the very few writers in Canada at the time who gave open and free expression to my appreciation of the merits of that book. It seemed to me to possess the seeds of genius. It was a much more virile and daring achievement in fiction than anything that had come from the pen of a Canadian author up to that time. Unfortunately, for Canada, it was greeted with a tirade of bigoted comment from those who ought to have been the first to recognize its merits. It was banned from many libraries. It was held up to scorn by many self-constituted critics, whose sole claim to be recognized as critics was the fact that they had secured a foothold with certain publications and were in a position to make themselves heard.

It was roundly denounced by a coterie of narrow-minded and short-sighted individuals who claimed to represent the conscience of the West. The author was never given a fair chance. His work was snowed under without any opportunity for him to defend himself, as he undoubtedly could have done, if he had been accorded anything like British fair play. Because he told the truth as he saw it, and because the truth was unpalatable to those who think it good that our young Canadian readers should be fed upon sugar and cream, and led to believe that everything in this Dominion is lovely and pure and perfect, Frederick Philip Grove was "turned down."

At that time I had occasional opportunities to express my opinion of his work in public lectures before various influential bodies, and it gave me a peculiarly keen pleasure to say precisely what I thought of the petty spirits who had done their best to kill a heroic and dauntless soul. They made no reply. They were content, in their smug self-righteousness, to remain silent. Perhaps they were wise. It is in any event a very pleasant task now to chronicle the fact that they did not kill the spirit that was in Frederick Philip Grove. They nearly drove him to wreck and ruin. They were almost responsible for his death, and they would have been his spiritual murderers if he had died. But he gathered sufficient moral courage to endure.

He has since written several important novels of the Canadian scene, and now at long last he gives us *In Search of Myself*, his life story. This is unquestionably one of the most absorbing and stimulating biographies ever penned by a Canadian author, for Mr. Grove, although he did not come to Canada until the end of the 19th century, has every right to be considered a Canadian author today.

. . . *In Search of Myself* is largely Mr. Grove's attempt to explain why in his opinion he has failed in what he set out to do—though I for one would regard it as rather an inspiring failure, if such an apparent contradiction of terms can be used. The section devoted to Mr. Grove's childhood is delightful. That covering his youth is adventure presented in a new and intensely intriguing manner. The second and larger half of the book is devoted to Mr. Grove's career in Canada. This will be found equally absorbing reading, not only to those interested in literature and literary workmanship, but to the general reading public. Those in particular who have followed Mr. Grove's literary career in this country will find here much that is of great value, both from an interpretive and an illuminative standpoint. . . .

S. Morgan-Powell, *The Montreal Daily Star*, October 12, 1946. By permission of *The Montreal Star*.

. . . Eminent literary folk may consider him the most accomplished among Canadian writers. But great fiction is more than the theme of the tale and one questions if Mr. Grove's characters generally are fairly representative of the Canadian scene.

As for this book it seems to put all events on an equal footing. They are not classified as major and minor, though most people will agree that the dislocation of one or two of the vertebrae is rather more important than the buying and using of a shaving brush. But the writing as writing, is excellent, and if you are interested in hard-luck stories this is ready-made for you.

J. E. Middleton, *Saturday Night*, October 19, 1946. By permission of *Saturday Night*.

. . . Grove's novels are so massive and compelling they actually force the reader to ignore some major weaknesses. The autobiography, with its lumbering and wandering style, produces much the same effect. Great autobiography should include much of the stubbornness, the mystery and the vastness of life (as, indeed, all important writing should); it is no place for the minor, polished and isolated talent. Grove's book reflects the awesome and wonderful majesty of man's struggle on earth. I think that *In Search of Myself* is a magnificent book.

I hope that many copies are sold, as a belated gesture to a man whose integrity deserved much more than Canadians were willing to give. I particularly hope—but do not really expect—that it will be read by all those intellectuals who have no sense of being Canadian, or anything else.

Robert Weaver, *The Varsity*, Toronto, October 21, 1946. By permission of Robert Weaver and *The Varsity*.

. . . In his autobiography, we have landscapes etched with the pencil of prose poetry; European, American and Canadian "interiors" not unworthy of a literary Rembrandt; philosophy matured with the years; exciting adventures by land and sea; and confessions of faith. Of F. P. Grove's work as he expounds it, and of his criticisms of the Canadian attitude to literature, much remains to be said.

W. J. Hurlow, *The Ottawa Citizen*, October 26, 1946. By permission of *The Ottawa Citizen*.

. . . As the title indicates, *In Search of Myself* is not a mere record, it is an attempt to put down on paper the development of a soul. In recounting his life's story, Grove has followed the technique of his novels, leading the reader on through developing a deepening understanding and appreciation of the principals [*sic*] of a personality, rather than through suspense or the building up of a plot.

It is well that he has followed that course in writing his autobiography. Comparatively few Canadians know his works well enough to be interested, at once, in what he accomplished or did not accomplish in the writing field. *In Search of Myself* stands on its own feet, as a revealing human document. . . .

Tom Brophey, *The Windsor Daily Star*, November 9, 1946. By permission of *The Windsor Star*.

Grove's autobiography is the year's most important contribution to the Canadian literary movement. Though it will not rank anywhere near the top in immediate popularity, it will probably be read longer than any other Canadian book of 1946. Having in it the same intimacy as *A Search for America*, his most popular novel, *In Search of Myself* will most likely far outsell any of the other six Grove novels. At 75, and in a critical physical condition, he has left us a moving narrative of unique interest. . . .

For Grove marks dramatically the shift of Canadian fiction from entertainment to social criticism, the maturing of Canadian literature. . . .

William A. Deacon, *The Globe and Mail*, November 2, 1946. By permission of *The Globe and Mail*, Toronto.

. . . Grove is a literary artist of a type recognized in Europe, but hardly guessed-at in Canada. Without attempting to relate the men in any other way, or to make a comparison between their writings, he resembles Thomas Mann in his philosophical approach to his work, in his scholarly background, in his integrity, and in his essentially European estimate of the place of the artist in the community. His books have few charms for the ordinary reader; he makes demands on emotion and understanding which the average patron of a lending-library cannot meet, and will not tolerate from a man who has not been labelled "great" by non-Canadian reviewers. He is chilly and austere; sometimes his books are "unpleasant," but not in the sniggering way that the public likes and the censor overlooks. He says himself: "The artist should always build his work as if it were meant to last through the centuries; and only the great commonplaces of life are worthy of being forever repeated and expounded anew." Is it surprising that this man's voice was drowned by the clamour of the literary hucksters in the market place? And will it be surprising if his voice is still heard two hundred years from now when Canada has begun to take intelligent pride in her literature? But the posthumous fame which he will surely enjoy can do nothing for the living man. . . .

"Samuel Marchbanks" (Robertson Davies), The Peterborough *Examiner*, November 6, 1946. By permission of Robertson Davies.

. . . It is an autobiography told beautifully and with great simplicity. That would have made it a notable book enough. But more than that it is the story of an intense and fabulous life—an adventure more varied and strange than fiction could ever be. . . .

"H.R.G.," *Winnipeg Free Press*, November 16, 1946. By permission of the *Winnipeg Free Press*.

In Search of Myself by Frederick Philip Grove is the autobiography of an eminent pioneering novelist who tried to make his living out of literature in Canada. It is therefore, as you might expect, a pretty melancholy hard-luck story.

Essentially Grove's book is an indictment. As a self-revelation, it is more important for what it tells of the slow and painful growth of a reading public in this Dominion of ours than for what it reveals about himself.

Those who have read Grove's bitter records of life on the prairies, *Settlers of the Marsh*, *Over Prairie Trails*, *Our Daily Bread*, and *A Search For America*, will find nothing here to surprise them. Through all his works, as in this one, there runs the same grim moodiness. His narrative is never lit by a spark of humor, and is as stark as the flat lands of wintry Saskatchewan.

Because of this one-sided austerity, Grove, it seems to me, was never a truly great writer. For it simply is not true to life that man battles against the elements in an atmosphere of sustained gloom.

The theme of nature's relentless mastery over the individual was more ably handled by Louis Hémon and Thomas Hardy, to mention only two. In every page of their novels of the soil, we never forget that man is a helpless thing, humble before the awful power of land and weather. Yet because the farmers stubbornly persist in good cheer, their plight becomes more real to us in its pathos, and we feel a spiritual kinship to them as humans.

Grove's chief distinction as a novelist was his intellectual sincerity. He was a poor craftsman. Yet no matter how rough-hewn, you felt that his prose was pieced together with tremendous effort, like an unwieldy mason scooping up mortar from his own flesh.

Aldous Huxley, of course, once commented that a bad book is as much of a labor to write as a good one; for it comes just as sincerely from the author's soul. But this smacks too much of surface cynicism. Rather I like to think that Grove was like Honoré Balzac or Theodore Dreiser. Like them, he sensed that he was an awkward writer. But he had the courage to keep polishing and repolishing his work, desperately hoping that a few flashes of brilliance would shine through the rough.

It is true, unfortunately, that Grove never achieved a *Père Goriot* or *An American Tragedy*, but at least he did more than any other Canadian writer during his period: against all opposition he was striving to be an honest creative artist.

This triple sense of frustration—frustrated by his ungainly writing ability, his prairie environment and his cold reception from the Canadian reading public—is sombrely reflected throughout *In Search of Myself*.

Frank Rasky, *The Vancouver Sun*, November 30, 1946. By permission of *The Vancouver Sun*.

. . . Grove is one of the most important of the few outstanding novelists Canada has produced. Now his autobiography is interesting to the far too few who are acquainted with his books. Undoubtedly the estimate of the years will give to Grove the place in literature he so richly deserves. His autobiography will then be of inestimable value in understanding the rare spirit of the man and the history of his times.

M. P. W., *Winnipeg Tribune*, December 14, 1946. By permission of the *Winnipeg Tribune*.

. . . It has been years since we were so moved by a book. Perhaps the last time one made such an impression upon us was when we read *The Grapes of Wrath*, although they had little in common except their terrific sincerity. . . .

Is Grove a great novelist? His autobiography provides no answer. That must be found in the novels themselves, but *In Search of Myself* is a great book; make no mistake about that. Perhaps the final answer rests with us who are readers. We are not yet worthy to be readers of men like Grove. That is why we condemn them to a lifelong struggle to make us hear.

J. V. McAree, *The Globe and Mail*, January 8, 1947. By permission of *The Globe and Mail*, Toronto.

It may sometimes occur to even the most ardent admirers of *A Search for America* to wonder whether Frederick Philip Grove the man—that granite figure upon which the storms of implacable fate have beaten in vain for forty years—may not outlive Frederick Philip Grove the novelist. Posterity can hardly fail to be interested in a life so continuously and profoundly at odds with the predominant forces of its era, especially if it turns out that the struggle was due to that life being prophetic of new forces to come. But posterity might conceivably cease to be interested in more than a few of the creations of Grove's imagination, not because they are not greatly imagined, but because they are not bodied forth in a great literary style.

Almost the whole of Grove's writing produces, to a singular degree, the impression of being a good translation of a much better original in some other language. Nor is that surprising. Grove is by origin the absolute European —neither English nor Scottish nor Scandinavian nor German nor French. The languages of half-a-dozen countries were his from earliest youth, with little preference between them. In a sense he has no mother tongue. His style has the clarity of a man writing with great care in a slightly foreign language, but not the beauty or the grandeur of a man writing in his own language which he passionately loves. The overmastering drive of literary creation as he describes it, and he describes it in this book very fully, seems to relate entirely to the visualizing of the characters and situations, not to the getting of them down in words, which in Grove's mind seems to be a journeyman's job not clearly distinguishable from the labour of typing the script.

. . . Whether Grove is a Canadian author is a matter of definition. He certainly elected of his own choice to do his writing in Canada. But he is not an author in the current Canadian tradition. At a time when Canadian literature is reacting from colonialism to an exaggerated nationalism he is a cosmopolitan and an ardent anti-nationalist. At a time when Canadian writers are still held down by the inhibitions of Victorianism (a Puritanism run to seed and decaying on the stalk) he practises the honest frankness of a continental Europe which never knew Puritanism—a very different thing from the exhibitionist frankness of the current American output. At a time when Canadian authors are called upon to depict the Canadian scene to the patriotic end that Canadians may

learn to understand it and to love it better, he depicts only
that part of it which imposes on mankind the bitterest
hardships in the struggle for survival. By this means he
has influenced Canadian literature, and much for its good,
by diverting it slightly from its too facile optimism. But
his proper function, obviously, was to reach the whole
audience of North America, not as a Canadian author but
as a North American one; and he was barred from doing
so by the unconquerable belief of the United States part
of that audience that nothing of importance could come
out of Canada except romances of the Mounted Police
and of the habitants, and that everything that could be
said about the frontier life had already been said by United
States writers.

   B. K. Sandwell, *University of Toronto Quarterly*, January, 1947, 202,
   205-6 By permission of University of Toronto Press.

Other reviews of *In Search of Myself* appeared in *The
Toronto Daily Star*, October 12, 1946; the *London Free
Press*, October 16, 1946; *Halifax Daily Star*, October 19,
1946; *The Telegraph-Journal*, Saint John, N.B., October
22, 1946; *Ottawa Journal*, October 26, 1946; *Montreal
Gazette*, November 2, 1946; *Vancouver Daily Province*,
November 16, 1946; *Echoes*, Spring 1947.

Consider Her Ways (1947)

. . . To read this book is to see afresh that many of the
dicta uttered about Grove's writing do not hold: for
example, that he keeps women in the background, being
unable to draw them; that he has written tragedies because
he himself is grim; that his style lapses when he attempts
imaginative writing. And aside from all that, the book
succeeds as a fantasy because the author continually
demands more and more of the imagination of his readers:
the climax is not reached even when we see an ant and a
human being reading together a human treatise on ants;

after that the ants observe, and mimic in their records, the Irish accent of the scrub-women who are on the point of annihilating them with disinfecting mops.

Though unlike his other books in many ways, this one is highly characteristic of Grove. He has always seen every activity in its social implications, and even in a cosmic significance. Here the style and tone is more characteristic of his conversation than of his other writing: the light hints of a vast scientific background and a whole world of literature, the continuous irony, the occasional quiet chuckle. It is Grove in a holiday mood; the composition was obviously an amusing experience for himself.

Carleton Stanley, *Winnipeg Free Press*, January 25, 1947. By permission of the *Winnipeg Free Press*.

. . . Read simply as adventure this book has something of the timeless fascination of such classics as *20,000 Leagues Under the Sea* and other fantastic excursions into a realm of which at the time nothing was known. Read as satire it will be found richly rewarding in places, and amusing throughout. The only complaint the average reader will have to find is that the book ends all too soon, so attached do we become to the valiant, shrewd, and wise Wawaquee, and so familiar do we feel with formicarian life. . . .

"P.P.," *The Montreal Daily Star*, January 25, 1947. By permission of *The Montreal Star*.

As always, the finished craftsmanship of Dr. Grove's latest book is striking. . . .

. . . When it is remembered that never before has Dr. Grove published anything light or purporting to be funny, it is remarkable that *Consider Her Ways* succeeds in its mood of delicate playfulness. Even the slightly antiquated diction helps to support the illusion that an ant is writing the record of her adventurous career.

True to himself, Dr. Grove has avoided the obvious, flippant wisecracks, which constitute popular contemporary humor. He sends readers to their dictionaries for the meanings of scientific terms relating to the physical structure of ants, their dwellings and habits; he never boggles at a word like pogonomyrmex, thus at once preserving an illusion of fiction and giving instruction in details of an intricate subject. Therefore he has once more, with great originality and finesse, written for the discerning and discriminating rather than for a mass reading audience.

The Globe and Mail, February 1, 1947 (unsigned). By permission of *The Globe and Mail, Toronto.*

. . . The satirical possibilities of the plan are almost unlimited, and Grove has exploited many of them. The book, unlike some of Grove's novels, is predominantly humorous, but the humour is ironic and biting. In the ants' secure conviction that they are the very apex of creation and that all other forms of life (including Man) were created to minister to their needs, Grove mocks at human pride in making the same assumption; in their solemn and smug investigation of other inferior and "primitive" tribes of ants he ridicules the condescending spirit in which, too often, our anthropological and sociological inquiries are conducted. The account of a slave-holding tribe of ants is used to satirize capitalism and war; another tribe has a peculiar caste of creatures which have obvious (and not very flattering) resemblances to authors and critics; and masses of ants die sordidly in their frantic efforts to acquire "the scent of royal favor."

All the foregoing examples are chosen from the indirect satire, in which the recording ant's observations of other ants are employed to hint more or less subtly at similar human perversities. But there is also a considerable amount (though less than we might hope) of direct satire, in which the wise old scholar-ant observes and comments on Man at first hand. Man's aggressive fierceness and universal destructiveness, his wastefulness, his abuse of reason to a low cunning, the irrationality of his language (especially its spelling), the peculiarity of his dress and the emphasis he places upon it, his tendency to prize least the most important labor, his insane hurry, his materialistic and mechanistic civilization—all these fall beneath Grove's satiric thong.

It is, then, a clever book. It is also an erudite one, in its scientific knowledge and accuracy reminding us of Melville's *Moby Dick*. For many readers, indeed, it will seem too erudite. One sentence reads: "Their workers are monomorphic though, as would be expected from their entomophagous habits, by no means small." One wishes that some of the fairly abstruse information about ants might have been eliminated and replaced by more of the direct satire on humanity. It is simply, I suppose, another proof of human self-centredness and pride, but the fact is that our interest in the book quickens whenever Man enters. And such is our loyalty to poor misguided *genus homo* that the effect of the satire, on this reviewer, was to make him rally to Man's defence against the cold, superior, all-wise probing of the ant's sharp poisonous gaster!

Desmond Pacey, *Toronto Daily Star*, February 8, 1947, 5. By permission of the *Toronto Daily Star*.

For sheer originality of setting and form this latest novel by Frederick Philip Grove stands on a plane apart from the great bulk of literature old and new. Indeed, although it tells a story right enough with a beginning, a middle and an end, it is not in essence a novel at all, any more than *Gulliver's Travels* is a novel. There is a curious similarity between Swift's and Grove's purpose, viewpoint and technique that is one of the more intriguing aspects of the book. . . .

Mr. Grove who, although he is a Canadian by choice, cannot in any true sense be called a Canadian author, has clearly something intriguing to say in *Consider Her Ways*. His cosmopolitan, supra-national outlook, his strong vein of philosophy, and his honest scholarship all are anchors to windward as his literary ship rides the stormy seas of public favor. But it must also be said that for sheer, unrelieved, relentlessly exhausting wordiness, he stands on a plane so far removed from the common would-be-read author that he is in grave danger of going down to posterity in a vacuum. Satire, particularly, cannot be successfully maintained without the light touch; and Grove's touch is much too reminiscent of the mallet to win him readers in quantity. True, an author does not have to write in a style that makes pleasant reading, but it helps a lot if he wants to be read—as Mr. Grove says authors, who are "notoriously vain," do.

Lydia Davison, *The Gazette*, Montreal, February 8, 1947.

. . . Now here is a book which really does mean something, written by one of the most neglected important writers of our time. No book club has seized upon it for wholesale distribution, but it will outlast many works which have been granted that equivocal distinction. Mr. Grove has written a book about men as men appear to ants, and the qualities of wit and fancy which have been discernible, under strict discipline, in his earliest works, are given free rein here. It may be that the satirical intent of the book will be too obscure for some readers but many others will cherish it. Here we have a fine mind amusing itself, and that always makes stimulating reading.

Robertson Davies, the Peterborough *Examiner*, February 26, 1947. By permission of Robertson Davies.

. . . *Consider Her Ways* labours through long sections of complex and clumsy prose. Much of the writing could, I am sure, have been drastically simplified without any loss of accuracy. The straight narrative sections are best, fast moving and often exciting. Grove succeeds in endowing his ants with character, and those are interesting and believable which correspond to the successful types in his novels (which means that a fair number are not). The satire itself is not uniformly successful; some sections are too fantastic (for instance, the description of the three surviving ants busily reading books in the New York public library); others are ponderous and dull, far too obvious (a description of ants called "authors" found in one colony). Grove attacks mainly false pride, materialism, stupid and unnecessary violence.

Unfortunately, early sections of the book are among the most slow moving ones, and I imagine some readers will immediately be put off. Later, there is a good deal of fascinating material. Still, while *Consider Her Ways* is often interesting and is certainly unique in relation to Grove's other work, I doubt if it will add much to his reputation.

Robert Weaver, *The Varsity*, March 7, 1947. By permission of Robert Weaver and *The Varsity*.

. . . Satire however is one of those forms of art in which one must be practically perfect or one does not succeed at all, and Frederick Philip Grove's *Consider Her Ways* is far from a perfect satire. Mr. Grove's trouble is that he expects a great deal of the human race and has been, and remains, bitterly disappointed. That is not the satirist's attitude. The satirist is not a disappointed man, he is a man who never, at least since he first came anywhere near being a satirist, has had any expectations about it, nor to do it good (Mr. Grove has both of these purposes) but simply to express a satiric feeling. As astounding fertility of imagination does indeed lend a measure of romantic interest to this tale of the great expedition of a Venezuelan ant-army to New York and its near annihilation in the Public Library on Fifth Avenue, but Mr. Grove's description of the author-ants (required to fast for the first quarter of their lives and often dying in the process) and the critic-ants (whose names are never inscribed on the roll of honour but are allowed to die with them) is about as near as he comes to "taking off" any aspect of human society. That such a vast amount of erudition about the Hymenoptera should be put to so little use is very regrettable. A purely scientific disquisition would have told us much more about ants and very little less about humans.

B. K. Sandwell, *Saturday Night*, April 26, 1947, 12. By permission of *Saturday Night*.

If there is in Canada one writer more than another whose career has proved that a prophet is not without honor save in his own country and among his own people it is Frederick Philip Grove. But Canadian readers are waking up. Happily for us, Mr. Grove still lives and continues to produce books marked by power and originality such as few of our other contemporary writers seem able to attain.

His recently published autobiography, *In Search of Myself*, is now followed by a work as far out of his own beaten track and the well worn paths pursued by others as it could possibly be. In it, he bids us consider the ways of the ant and be wise. . . .

The Ottawa Evening Citizen, July 26, 1947 (unsigned). By permission of *The Ottawa Citizen*.

. . . *Consider Her Ways* is a masterpiece of its kind. Certainly only an intelligence of the highest order, coupled with an inordinate capacity for study, could produce it. The reader's reaction to the book will depend upon what kind of masterpiece he likes.

"M. P.," *The Winnipeg Tribune*, September 20, 1947. By permission of *The Winnipeg Tribune*.

. . . *Consider Their Ways* [*sic*] compresses much myrmecological information into a book that seems to be half scientific romance and half a satirical voyage. Even if the book clearly belonged in this survey, it would not constitute a notable contribution to the fiction of the year; for it achieves distinction only in a few sombrely satirical passages, in which a serious writer distils his bitterness toward a society that, he feels, has not given him his due meed of praise.

Claude T. Bissell, *University of Toronto Quarterly*, April, 1948, 277. By permission of the University of Toronto Press.

Reviews of *Consider Her Ways* also appeared in *The Telegraph-Journal*, Saint John, N.B., February 8, 1947; *Halifax Chronicle*, February 22, 1947; *Vancouver Daily Province*, February 22, 1947; *Victoria Daily Colonist*, February 23, 1947; *Hamilton Spectator*, March 29, 1947; *Dalhousie Review*, XXVII (April, 1947). 116-117: *The Narrator*, April, 1947.

THREE OBITUARY TRIBUTES

CANADIAN DREISER

NORTHROP FRYE

Frederick Philip Grove was certainly the most serious of Canadian prose writers, and may well have been the most important one also. His first book was published in 1922, when he was fifty. If he had understood the mechanics of preparing manuscripts for publication, he might have been in print thirty years earlier, in which case he would have pioneered in realistic fiction along with Dreiser. He is best known for his novels, *The Yoke of Life, Settlers of the Marsh, Two Generations, Fruits of the Earth,* and above all, *Our Daily Bread* and the comparatively recent *The Master of the Mill.* Next in importance come his auto-biographical studies, *In Search of America* and *In Search of Myself,* then his narrative and descriptive essays, *Over Prairie Trails* and *The Turn of the Year.* There is a full-length critical study of him by Desmond Pacey. Many of his books are out of print, and it is easy to pick up a hearsay impression that he wrote nothing but gloomy epics on the "no fun on the farm" theme. Those who read him, however, will find that he not only reads very well, but is full of surprising insights and an unflagging sincerity and power.

Like many Canadian writers, he has a significance for Canadians that is difficult to share with other countries. Perhaps it is only to the Canadian reader that his faults seem to be, not only inseparable from his virtues, but curiously instructive in themselves. His life is a pitiful record of frustration and heartbreak, combined with a

In *The Canadian Forum,* September, 1948, 121-2. By permission of Northrop Frye.

dogged insistence on writing as he felt without compromise. He is perhaps our only example of an artist who made his whole life a drama of the artist's fight for survival in an indifferent society. Yet one cannot help wondering how far his integrity merged with a self-conscious pose of integrity, how much of his frustration sprang out of an obscure but profound will to be frustrated. No one can answer such a question either about oneself or others, and the question would seem impudent if even the novels did not show a conflict between integrity and something else. A fine flash of ribald comedy may be smothered by a distrust of humor far deeper than prudery, or the logical development of a scene may be suddenly twisted into moralizing. There is something profoundly Canadian about this fear of letting oneself go, and Grove speaks for a whole era of Canadian literature when he says ("Apologia pro Vita et Opere suo" in *The Canadian Forum* for August, 1931): "We (the artists) aim at creating that which will live beyond Christianity and in spite of whatever sublimation may take its place. We shall most certainly fail in that; for . . . this is not a time for the production of great art; but we are content to be the forerunners of such a time; and, to say it once more, we are not much concerned about our ultimate failure or success. Failure may be tragic; but we do not shrink from tragedy." As Christianity would say, the time is at hand.

AN EDITOR'S TRIBUTE

LORNE PIERCE

In 1940, when Frederick Philip Grove was sixty-nine, he wrote his publisher: "I'm fighting in the last ditch." "Glad you like the Ant-Book. How did I come to stumble on to that theme? Well, I have always been a student of ants; and I was an ant myself, was I not, in the great American formicary. . . . No, my work did not grow out of the milieu of what was being done by others in Canada. I neither knew of it nor cared for it. That a few of them, of late, have sought me out is no matter." Much of his life Grove had lived in an isolation which, in a later day, he compared to that of "an Antarctic explorer lost on the Barrier who, at the best, meets a scavenger gull." Summing it all up he regarded himself as a tragic failure. "To have tried greatly and to have failed greatly, that," said Grove, "was tragedy." Again he said: "I, the cosmopolitan, had fitted myself to be the spokesman of a race." Why had he failed? All his life Grove believed that he was born an unwanted child, and that he remained unwanted wherever he went. Now and then he seems to suggest that the tragedy was in himself, following his Greek masters. "We can but become what we are." Although Grove wrote two long books which had for their main theme his search for himself, he failed to understand his own world and his own times, much less understand himself.

Frederick Philip Grove was born in Russia, February

"Frederick Philip Grove (1871-1948)" by Lorne Pierce, in the *Royal Society of Canada, Transactions and Proceedings*, XLIII (1949), 113-119. Reprinted by permission of the Royal Society of Canada.

14, 1871, while his parents were returning to their home in Sweden. His forbears were born in England, Scotland and Sweden. For the first twelve years of his life, his parents being estranged, Grove travelled about Europe with his mother, his seven sisters remaining under the care of his father in Sweden. He attended school as he moved about and studied under tutors. Then, in 1887, tragedy struck. His beautiful and brilliant mother died, and for a quarter of a century he wandered about the world a lonely man. At the Hamburg Gymnasium (1888) he was awarded a four-year scholarship. Grove hoped to use his scholarship at the Sorbonne, but chance caused him to join Lord Rutherford, his mother's uncle, and he set out upon a scientific expedition to Siberia. A year later he cruised in his yacht along the shores of the Mediterranean, and entered the Sorbonne (hesitating between medicine and archaeology). During the winter of 1889 Grove wandered through the Sahara, and matriculated at the University of Rome. He studied later at the Imperial German Institute of Archaeology. In 1891 and 1892 Grove was in Madagascar, South Africa, New Zealand, attended lectures for a time at the University of Munich, and then, in the spring of 1892, sold his yacht and visited the United States and Canada. While in America Grove received word that his father had become bankrupt, and for a time he wandered through America living a vagabond life and acquiring an eclectic philosophy of art and life.

In the autumn of 1893 Grove reached Winnipeg and for two years worked on Manitoba farms. Here he began his memoirs. For almost eighteen years, from 1894 to 1912, Grove drifted about, farming, working his way to Europe five winters on cattle boats, visiting Rome in quest of archaeological data, wandering in Canada and Venezuela, studying the ant. Then in 1912 he returned to Manitoba, his spiritual home, the place in all the world that reminded him of the steppes of Siberia. Here he became a school teacher, married, by great good fortune, a fellow teacher, Miss Catherine Wiens, in 1914, and set out upon his odyssey as a writer.

Grove has said that all life is meeting, that meeting was the very essence of the matter. Certainly Grove had been fortunate above most of those who wrote in Canada because of the interesting places and people he had known. He not only knew the masterpieces in the English, French, German, and Italian and Swedish languages, but was at home in the Golden Age of Greece and the Silver Age of Rome—most of all at home in Greece. In Paris he knew Gide, Verlaine, Mallarmé, Heredia and others who were in their turn to become classics. Whether his contacts with the myriad new scenes and with the crowding new faces were too brief or too casual to leave any distinct impression, it is true that in none of his books has he left a commentary upon an eminent man or important town that reveals any flashing insight, any fresh probing of a man or his milieu that we desire to remember.

Perhaps it was because the chief object of his search was after all himself, the only thing that mattered to him, just as in all his novels the principal male character is a reflection of some aspect of his own character. It may be that as we fail to comprehend men and the currents of the times about us, we also fail to understand what goes on within us. There is no overwhelming belief in anything outside himself, no overmastering love, no ineffable name, and no sanctuary. He plods patiently from detail to detail, slaving at his accumulation of data, indomitable in writing and rewriting, but somehow failing to seize the core of the matter.

His tragic view of life did not so much derive from the Greeks, as from the lack of an overmastering passion that drove him out beyond himself, a sublime faith. This was the reason for the sense of futility that came in time to weigh him down and overwhelm him in bitterness. All life is conflict: man against hostile Fate, against unfriendly Nature, against the menacing advance of Time; parent against child, man against woman; the deathless dream of greatness, with no armour but courage, and the end failure and despair. Why? Grove had no answer. Grove held that the artist with his insights and experiences must meet his audience before his art is complete. That he regarded as the final irony of his own life. He and his audience had failed to meet; his books hardly sold at all, many of his MSS could not find a publisher. Then ill health dogged him, and deafness shut him off increasingly. "If I were to follow my own inclination, I'd go on the road, in spite of desperately ill health; for most of the time I feel that, if I were a dog, I'd sit down on my haunches and howl with my pains."

In 1921 Grove completed his work for the B.A. at the University of Manitoba and was appointed to a better school. In 1922, ten years after his return to Manitoba, Grove at last published a book. *Over Prairie Trails* is the ripe fruit of the long drives Grove made to and from his school, his reading of Thoreau and Burroughs, and his almost mystical contemplation of the prairies at all hours and under all weathers. Grove once described art as "essentially the activity of the human soul," feeling that it derives its immortality from that. Everything of value in art or life was bound up with humanity. The foundation of all life was human nature. So it is that in this book of nature essays, and its companion *The Turn of the Year* (1923), Grove not only achieves some of his most memorable descriptions but, at the same time, presents one of the most revealing disclosures of his own mind and heart. His sincerity and sanity, his integrity both as artist and man, the hard clean core of his fine intelligence, are here revealed for all to see.

Settlers of the Marsh (1925) announced the appearance of a Canadian novelist who would thereafter have to be reckoned with. It dealt with the problem of personal suffering, a problem often to appear in Grove's work, and one that he hoped to deal with comprehensively and adequately in his last great book, "The Seasons"—never to see the light of day. The furore following the publication of *Settlers of the Marsh* deprived him of his school, and, as once before in sickness, he was supported by his valiant wife. With the publication of *In Search of America* (1927), an autobiographical novel, Grove's position as a leading Canadian author was secure. Then at the height of his popularity *Our Daily Bread* (1928) appeared, regarded by many as his best novel. A lecture tour resulted in a collection of addresses entitled *It Needs to be Said* (1929), in which Grove discourses upon the plight of Canadian fiction, on democracy, education and kindred matters. He appeared as a crusader, something of a prophet and reformer, and essayed to be a spokesman for his race in a limited way. His cosmopolitanism prevented him from becoming sentimental and naive. As always he is serious, revealing little humour but a good deal of irony. Irony was his most trusted weapon.

For the next two years Grove was associated, as editor, with the Graphic Press, Ottawa, an unfortunate venture that depleted his slender financial resources and placed a tragic strain upon his frail health. In 1930 *The Yoke of Life*, one of his most successful novels, was published and his son was born. Three years before his only daughter had died. The following year he purchased a small farm near Simcoe, Ontario, and managed it until 1938. His wife opened a private school in their spacious house, and during the last years she was again the main support of her home.

Grove contributed a number of short stories, poems and essays to Canadian periodicals, chiefly the university quarterlies, of which the autobiographical essays are the best and pave the way for his memoirs, *In Search of Myself* (1946).

With *Fruits of the Earth* (1933), one of his three best books, Grove took leave of the Canadian West and placed his characters over against a rural Ontario background.

Two Generations (1939), with this setting, brought nothing particularly new to the Canadian novel, while its understanding of Ontario and its people was not impressive. Grove often sounds like an outsider. Even where he is most at home, in his Western novels, not infrequently he seems at times to be translating into English, and to be observing the scene before him from a great distance. This is even more obvious in his Ontario novels. He treats his characters always with respect but not always with understanding, and while there is no flippancy or coyness there is often little subtlety or swift insight. Especially is this true of his women characters, who are rarely portrayed with success. However, only *The Master of the Mill* can be said to be a failure. It is melodramatic and unreal. His determination to tell all results in his saying little. Where he has usually avoided sentimentality he gave way entirely, losing not only the humour that had once saved him, but even his irony. His last book, *Consider Her Ways* (1947), sums up what he had been thinking about the ant, an interesting work partly scientific, partly allegorical—something of a homily on man and fate. When the end came several book-length MSS remained unpublished, and the tragedy was that the general indifference of the public to Grove's work offered little hope that publishers would compete for the honour of offering those MSS to the world. But their time will come.

A few honours came to Frederick Philip Grove and those arrived almost too late. The recognition which he confessed gave him special pleasure was the Gold Medal of the Royal Society of Canada (1934), in recognition of his long and distinguished contribution to Canadian literature. In 1941 he was elected a Fellow of the Royal Society. The University of Manitoba conferred upon him the Litt.D., and the University of Western Ontario the LL.D. Some day a competent editor will perform a final service to Grove's memory, namely, the preparation of a one-volume selection of the best of his work. There the general reader will find some hint of the greatness that was in Grove, the quality of the man. In a day of slipshod work, when sentimentality took the place of honest feeling, and prejudice did service for thought, Grove stood out like a mountain peak because of his integrity. While he lived and suffered, and slaved at his laborious composition, it was impossible for any conscientious Canadian writer to take the easy way out with his craft. He moved through life with great dignity under all circumstances, and raised the vocation of authorship in Canada to a new height. Frederick Philip Grove, like most men, was not always and everywhere great, but he was great often enough and in enough ways to make his name survive in the history of Canadian letters. His best memorial is his own words: "No man is born great; he becomes so."

"HERE HE LIES WHERE HE LONGED. . . ."

KAY ROWE

Dr. Frederick Philip Grove died of cerebral haemorrhage at Simcoe, Ontario, on August 19th of this year. In accordance with his last wishes, the body was shipped back to the Prairies for burial in a country churchyard one mile east of the village of Rapid City beside the grave of May Grove, deceased 1927, age 12 years.

The casket arrived from the east at the railway point nearest Rapid City. This is the dot designated on the railway maps as "North Brandon" . . . nine miles north of the City of Brandon. It's nothing but a railway station and freight shed in the midst of a sea of waving prairie grass in summer and a flat, white world of snow in winter. The transcontinental C.N.R. trains pound past the station twice a day moving east and west and stop for a scant three minutes to serve the Brandon City passenger trade. It was to this place, lonely and beautiful in late August, that Dr. Grove came back to the prairies to be laid in earth.

The hearse from Brandon carried the remains over the straight, flat roads the twenty miles to Rapid City. The stooked fields were rich with harvest and through the meadow grasses the lonely west wind moved with slow grace. The sole car which formed the funeral cortege contained two adults, near to tears, who talked intermittently of Dr. Pacey's book on Grove and speculated as to the location of the house in Brandon where Grove had lived one winter during his farm-hand days in the '90s.

Manitoba Arts Review, Spring, 1949, 62-4. By permission of Kay Rowe and the Arts Council, University of Manitoba.

Rapid City wore the indolent, secret atmosphere of all small towns in the August heat; the impression of life going on behind closed front doors out of the alien sight of strangers. Over by the Little Saskatchewan River is the neat, two-storied house where the Grove family lived for nearly five of their seven years in the town. They were happy in that house in spite of the spinal injury which necessitated his resignation as school principal. Mrs. Grove taught in the public school and young daughter, May, a pale, sweet child, played in the tangled garden. She could talk French and Latin at an age when her schoolmates were beginning to learn long division. Grove kept on writing. He drew forth the battered manuscripts started as early as 1892. They were ponderous affairs, written in long hand on both sides of the paper, sad with the ignominy of repeated rejections. But four of his books were published within their seven years' residence in Rapid City: *Over Prairie Trails, The Turn of the Year, Settlers of the Marsh* and *In Search of America*. Success went along with tragedy for it was during these seven abundant years that Grove suffered the serious fall which aggravated his old spinal injury and resulted in his spending sixteen months flat on his back. This was followed by a shattering blow in 1927 of the death of twelve-year-old May, from a ruptured appendix.

The cemetery stands on a hill-top a mile east of town, the neat stones enclosed by a fence of spruce trees overlooking the entire river valley. Dates on the stones cover the life spans of men and women who came to build this community as early as 1874. In the south-west corner is a small, marble headstone which marks the resting place of May Grove. The inscription is not from Holy Writ but are the transposed lines of Shelley on young Keats:

She is a portion of the loveliness
Which once she made more lovely. . . .

Her father was placed beside her. The officiating student theologian read the ancient, noble words in a clear, young voice. The sky vaulted vast, blue, cloudless. The butterflies were yellow with late summer. The twenty mourners listened. They were matrons who had "gone to school" to Mrs. Grove, her brother, old family friends who had kept in touch during the intervening two decades—some had visited the author and his wife at their farm near Simcoe, Ontario; a professor of English literature from Winnipeg; a representative from the teachers' society and three members of the local school board who had long recognized Grove's estimable contribution to teaching. After the service they gathered in small groups to talk of the man who had coloured their own lives. Then they jumped into their cars and drove back to town to tend drug store, sell farm machinery, write next Sunday's sermon or continue cutting up cukes for pickles.

"What was Frederick Philip Grove like as a person?" we asked one of the townsmen; an alert old boy, bright blue of eye and his tongue still heavy with a North England accent after fifty years in Western Canada.

"He was a dour kind of fellow—never much for talking. Always seemed to have his mind working inside itself. He wasn't what you'd ever call popular, neither! He wasn't affable, was never one to stop and pass the time o' day. Like as not when he did talk, in that careful, clipped kind of way, he'd say something pretty sharp—so sharp it cut, often. And he wouldn't join anything . . . hated meetings of any kind. I remember how he'd stand up to the school board. He didn't understand us and we didn't understand him. He was always fighting for more things for the school; always wanting more science equipment, more books for the library. He said that books were food for the mind and just as important as beef and milk for growing bodies."

"Was he a good teacher?"

"Never was any better than Grove . . . unless it was Mrs. Grove. Anybody around here'll say that! He was a man of true learning. Learning and teaching and writing was all that interested him. His idea of a good time, of a holiday, was to go tramping over the fields with May and Mrs. Grove. They'd bring home a basket full of the derndest things: those little green garter snakes, alive! those orange toadstools, the white fungus that grows in the wounds of old trees, birds' feathers and queer stones from the brook's edge. He'd study that kind of thing all the time. Nights I'd meet him walking down the river road with his head tilted right back on his spine, looking up at the stars. He knew where all the constellations sat at different seasons—could point out the planets and tell their names . . . just like I know the farms around here and who runs 'em. He'd travelled, too! All over the world! He'd been to Australia, to every country in Europe and once he was in the Sahara desert. He criss-crossed America and Canada a dozen times."

"What did he look like?"

"First thing you'd notice about him was his height. He stood about six-two and was always rake thin. He had sandy hair and while you wouldn't call him handsome—still—it was a face you'd never forget. It was a thinking face—with a high, thin nose and a strong mouth and eyes that never missed a thing even when he was doing algebra problems in his head."

"Did you ever read any of his books?"

"No! Never have much time for reading. But the Missus used to buy them in Winnipeg—she's got quite a collection now—he finally had about thirteen books published. She read 'em all—said they were depressing—they never had a happy ending. But I guess he must have pleased some people because those professors from Wesley College were always coming out to see him, helping him to sell more of his books and inviting him to talk to clubs in the big cities. . . ."

The late Dr. Frederick Philip Grove wandered down the byroads of four continents, watched stars move across the sky, the ways of plants and animals. His mind was a lonely hunter through the intricate mazes of the words of seven languages, through the secret places of the human heart. It is a privilege to recall in parting that he chose Canada as the place in which to live, to teach, to create and finally to lie in its rich, prairie earth.

A BIBLIOGRAPHY OF
FREDERICK PHILIP GROVE

A. **Books**

Over Prairie Trails, Toronto: McClelland and Stewart, 1922. Reprinted, 1923. Reissued, 1949. New Canadian Library edition, with introduction by Malcolm Ross, 1957.

The Turn of the Year, Toronto: McClelland and Stewart, 1923. Reissued, 1929.

Settlers of the Marsh, Toronto: Ryerson Press; New York: Doran, 1925. Cheap edition, 1927. New Canadian Library edition, with introduction by Thomas Saunders, 1966.

A Search for America, Ottawa: Graphic, 1927. Reprinted, June, 1928. Montreal and New York: Louis Carrier, 1928. London: Brentano, 1929.

Our Daily Bread, New York and Toronto: Macmillan, 1928. London: Jonathan Cape, 1928.

It Needs to be Said, Toronto: Macmillan, 1929.

The Yoke of Life, New York and Toronto: Macmillan, 1930. Trade edition, 1931.

Fruits of the Earth, London and Toronto: Dent, 1933. Reprinted, 1942. New Canadian Library edition, with introduction by M. G. Parks, 1965.

Two Generations, Toronto: Ryerson, 1939. Reprinted 1942.

The Master of the Mill, Toronto: Macmillan, 1944. New Canadian Library edition, with introduction by R. E. Watters, 1961.

In Search of Myself, Toronto: Macmillan, 1946.

Consider Her Ways, Toronto: Macmillan, 1947.

B. **Periodicals**

1. Short Stories and Sketches

   Twenty-three short stories and sketches were published in the *Winnipeg Tribune Magazine* between October 9, 1926 and April 23, 1927:

   "Thy Gypsy Trail" (Oct. 9, 1926), p. 8.

   "Camping in Manitoba" (Nov. 20, 1926), p. 12 (with photo of the Grove family camping).

   "North of Fifty-Three" (Part 1), (Nov. 27, 1926), p. 12.

   "Captain Harper's Last Voyage" (Part II of "North of Fifty-Three"), (Dec. 4, 1926), p. 12.

   "Lost" (Dec. 11, 1926), p. 12.

   "A Christmas in the Canadian Bush" (Dec. 18, 1926), p. 12.

   "The Boat" (Dec. 24, 1926), p. 12.

   "That Reminds Me" (Dec. 31, 1926), p. 12.

"A Hero of the Flu" (Jan. 15, 1927), p. 7.

"Prairie Character Studies: The Agent" (Jan. 22, 1927), p. 12.

"Prairie Character Studies: The Sale" (Jan. 29, 1927), p. 12.

"Prairie Character Studies: The Immigrant" (Feb. 5, 1927), p. 12.

"Dave Chisholm Entertains" (Feb. 12, 1927), p. 12.

"The Flood" (Feb. 19, 1927), p. 12.

"Dave Chisholm, 'The Goat' " (Feb. 26, 1927), p. 12.

"A First Night on Canadian Soil" (March 5, 1927), p. 12. (The first of three excerpts from *A Search for America*.)

" 'Beating It In' " (March 12, 1927), p. 12. (The second excerpt from *A Search for America*.)

"Hobos" (March 19, 1927), p. 12. (The third excerpt from *A Search for America*.)

"Water" (March 16, 1927), p. 12.

"Lazybones" (April 2, 1927), p. 12. Later published in *Queen's Quarterly*, LI (Summer, 1944), 162-73.

"The 'Dead-Beat' " (April 9, 1927), p. 12.

"Bachelors All" (April 16, 1927), p. 12.

"Relief" (April 23, 1927), p. 12.

Other stories were published as follows

"A Poor Defenceless Widow," *Saturday Night*, Jan. 9, 1932.

"Snow," *Queen's Quarterly*, XXXIX: 99-110 (Spring 1932).

"Riders," *Canadian Forum*, XIV: 177-178 (Feb. 1934).

"Platinum Watch," *Canadian Bookman*, XXI: 5-12 (Oct. 1939).

"The Desert," *Queen's Quarterly*, XLVIII: 216-232 (Autumn 1941).

"Lazybones," *Queen's Quarterly*, LI: 162-173 (Summer 1944).

2. Poems

"Indian Summer," *Canadian Forum*, X: 56 (Nov. 1929).

"Palinode," *Canadian Forum*, X: 444 (Sept. 1930).

"Dirge," *Canadian Forum*, XII: 257-261 (April 1932).

3. Autobiographical Essays

"Apologia pro vita et opere sua," *Canadian Forum*, XI: 420-422 (Aug. 1931).

"In Search of Myself," *University of Toronto Quarterly*, X: 60-67 (Oct. 1940).

"Postscript to *A Search for America*," *Queen's Quarterly*, XLIX: 197-213 (Autumn 1942).

4. Literary Criticism

"Realism and After," *Canadian Bookman,* Nov. 1928.

"A Writer's Classification of Writers," *University of Toronto Quarterly,* I: 236-253 (Jan. 1932).

"Thomas Hardy," *University of Toronto Quarterly,* I: 490-507 (July, 1932).

"The Plight of Canadian Fiction? A Reply," *University of Toronto Quarterly,* VII: 451-467 (July 1938).

(A reply to a previous article by Morley Callaghan.)

"Peasant Poetry and Fiction from Hesiod to Hémon," Royal Society of Canada *Transactions* II (1944), 89-98.

"Morality in the Forsyte Saga," *University of Toronto Quarterly,* XV (Oct. 1945), 54-64.

5. General

"The Flat Prairie," *Dalhousie Review,* XI: 213-216 (July 1938).

"Democracy and Education," *University of Toronto Quarterly,* XII: 389-402 (July 1943).